"KEEP YOURSELVES IN GOD'S LOVE"

THIS BOOK IS THE PROPERTY OF

_____

Photo Credits: ■ Page 14: © COMSTOCK Images/age fotostock ■ Page 134: Mixa/age fotostock ■ Page 201: © bilderlounge/Tips RF/age fotostock

© 2008
Watch Tower Bible and Tract Society of Pennsylvania
All Rights Reserved

PUBLISHERS
Watchtower Bible and Tract Society of New York, Inc.
Brooklyn, New York, U.S.A.

2008 Printing

This publication is provided as part of a worldwide Bible educational work supported by voluntary donations.

Unless otherwise indicated, Scripture quotations are from the modern-language
New World Translation of the Holy Scriptures—With References

"Keep Yourselves in God's Love"
English (*lv*-E)

Made in the United States of America

CONTENTS

CHAPTER	PAGE
1. "This Is What the Love of God Means"	5
2. How Can You Maintain a Good Conscience?	14
3. Love Those Whom God Loves	25
4. Why Respect Authority?	36
5. How to Keep Separate From the World	50
6. How to Choose Wholesome Entertainment	62
7. Do You Value Life as God Does?	74
8. God Loves Clean People	86
9. "Flee From Fornication"	97
10. Marriage—A Gift From a Loving God	110
11. "Let Marriage Be Honorable"	121
12. Speak What "Is Good for Building Up"	133
13. Celebrations That Displease God	144
14. Be Honest in All Things	160
15. See Good for Your Hard Work	171
16. Oppose the Devil and His Crafty Acts	183
17. "Building Up Yourselves on Your Most Holy Faith"	196
Appendix	206

Dear Lover of Jehovah:

"You will know the truth, and the truth will set you free," said Jesus. (John 8:32) How encouraging those words are! Yes, it is possible to know the truth, even in these critical "last days" when falsehood and untruth abound. (2 Timothy 3:1) Do you remember when you first recognized the truth as explained in God's Word? What a thrilling experience that was!

However, as important as it is to have an accurate knowledge of the truth and to have a regular share in telling others about it, we must also conduct ourselves in harmony with the truth. To do that, we need to keep ourselves in God's love. What does this involve? Jesus' words on the night before his death answer this question. He told his faithful apostles: "If you observe my commandments, you will remain in my love, just as I have observed the commandments of the Father and remain in his love."—John 15:10.

Notice that Jesus remained in God's love by observing his Father's commandments. The same is true of us today. To remain in God's love, we need to apply the truth in everyday life. That same evening, Jesus said: "If you know these things, happy you are if you do them." —John 13:17.

It is our sincere hope that this publication will help you to continue to apply the truth in your life and thus keep yourself "in God's love . . . with everlasting life in view."—Jude 21.

Governing Body of Jehovah's Witnesses

CHAPTER 1

"This Is What the Love of God Means"

"This is what the love of God means, that we observe his commandments; and yet his commandments are not burdensome."—1 JOHN 5:3.

DO YOU love God? If you have come into a dedicated relationship with Jehovah God, your answer surely is an emphatic yes—and rightly so! It is only natural for us to love Jehovah. Our love for God is really in response to his love for us. The Bible puts it this way: "As for us, we love, because he [Jehovah] first loved us."—1 John 4:19.

[2] Jehovah has taken the initiative to express his love for us. He provides us with a beautiful earthly home. He cares for our physical and material needs. (Matthew 5:43-48) More important, he looks after our spiritual needs. He gives us his Word, the Bible. In addition, he invites us to pray to him with the assurance that he will hear us and will give us his holy spirit to help us. (Psalm 65:2; Luke 11:13) Above all, he sent his most precious Son to be our Ransomer so that we might be delivered from sin and death. What great love Jehovah has shown to us!—John 3:16; Romans 5:8.

[3] Jehovah wants us to benefit from his love forever.

1, 2. What motivates you to love Jehovah God?
3. (a) To remain in God's love, what is required on our part? (b) What important question do we need to consider, and where is the answer found?

Dedication and baptism mark the beginning of a life of loving obedience to Jehovah

Whether we will or not, however, is really up to us. God's Word admonishes us: "Keep yourselves in God's love . . . with everlasting life in view." (Jude 21) The phrase "keep yourselves" suggests that to remain in God's love, action on our part is required. We need to respond to his love in concrete ways. An important question for us to consider, then, is this, 'How can I demonstrate my love for God?' The answer is found in the inspired words of the apostle John: "This is what the love of God means, that we observe his commandments; and yet his commandments are not burdensome." (1 John 5:3) We do well to examine carefully the meaning of these words, for we want to show our God just how much we love him.

"THIS IS WHAT THE LOVE OF GOD MEANS"

⁴ "The love of God"—what did the apostle John have in mind when he penned those words? This expression refers, not to God's love for us, but to our love for him. Can you recall when love for Jehovah began to grow in your heart?

⁵ Reflect, for a moment, on when you first learned the truth about Jehovah and his purposes and you began to exercise faith. You came to understand that although you were born a sinner alienated from God, Jehovah through Christ opened the way for you to attain the perfection that Adam lost and to inherit everlasting life. (Matthew 20:28; Romans 5:12, 18) You began to appreciate the magnitude of the sacrifice Jehovah made in sending his most precious Son to die for you. Your heart was moved, and you began to feel a love for the God who has shown such great love for you.—1 John 4:9, 10.

⁶ That feeling, however, was but the beginning of genuine love for Jehovah. Love is not just a feeling; nor is it a matter of mere words. True love for God involves more than simply saying, "I love Jehovah." Like faith, genuine love is defined and characterized by the actions it prompts. (James 2:26) Specifically, love expresses itself in deeds pleasing to the one who is loved. Hence, when love for Jehovah took root in your heart, you were moved to want to live in a way that pleases your

---

4, 5. (a) To what does the expression "the love of God" refer? (b) Describe how love for Jehovah began to grow in your heart.
6. How is genuine love expressed, and what did love for God move you to do?

heavenly Father. Are you a baptized Witness? If so, this deep affection and devotion caused you to make the most important decision of your life. You dedicated yourself to Jehovah to do his will, and you symbolized your dedication by getting baptized. (Romans 14:7, 8) Fulfilling this solemn promise to Jehovah involves what the apostle John next mentions.

"WE OBSERVE HIS COMMANDMENTS"

7 John explains what the love of God means: "We observe his commandments." What are God's commandments? Jehovah gives us a number of specific commands through his Word, the Bible. For example, he forbids such practices as drunkenness, fornication, idolatry, stealing, and lying. (1 Corinthians 5:11; 6:18; 10:14; Ephesians 4:28; Colossians 3:9) Observing God's commandments involves living in harmony with the Bible's clear moral standards.

8 To please Jehovah, however, we need to do more than just obey his direct commands. Jehovah does not hem us in with laws governing every aspect of our daily life. Hence, in the course of each day, we may encounter many situations for which there are no specific Bible commands. In such cases, how can we know what will be pleasing to Jehovah? The Bible contains clear indications of God's way of thinking. As we study the Bible, we learn what Jehovah loves and what he hates. (Psalm 97:10; Proverbs 6:16-19) We come to discern attitudes and actions that he values. The more we learn about

---

7. What are some of God's commandments, and what does observing these involve?
8, 9. How can we know what is pleasing to Jehovah even in situations where there is no direct Bible law? Give an example.

"This Is What the Love of God Means"

Jehovah's personality and ways, the more we will be able to let his thinking mold our decisions and influence our actions. Thus, even in situations where there is no specific Bible law, we can often perceive "what the will of Jehovah is."—Ephesians 5:17.

⁹ For example, the Bible contains no direct command telling us not to watch movies or TV programs that feature gross violence or sexual immorality. But do we really need a specific law against watching such things? We know how Jehovah views these matters. His Word plainly tells us: "Anyone loving violence [Jehovah's] soul certainly hates." (Psalm 11:5) It also says: "God will judge fornicators and adulterers." (Hebrews 13:4) By reflecting on those inspired words, we can clearly perceive what the will of Jehovah is. We therefore choose not to be entertained by watching graphic portrayals of the sort of practices that our God hates. We know that it pleases Jehovah when we avoid the moral filth that this world tries to pass off as harmless entertainment.*

¹⁰ What is the primary reason that we observe God's commandments? Why do we want to live each day in harmony with what we know to be God's way of thinking? We do not choose such a course simply to escape punishment or to avoid the harmful consequences that come to those who ignore God's will. (Galatians 6:7) Instead, we view obedience to Jehovah as a precious opportunity to show our love for him. Just as a child is eager to win his father's smile of approval, so we want to win Jehovah's approval. (Psalm 5:12) He is our

---

* See Chapter 6 of this publication for a discussion of how to choose wholesome entertainment.

10, 11. Why do we choose a course of obedience to Jehovah, and what sort of obedience do we give him?

Father, and we love him. Nothing brings us greater joy or deeper satisfaction than knowing that we are living in a way that "gets approval from Jehovah."—Proverbs 12:2.

¹¹ Our obedience, then, is not given begrudgingly; nor is it selective or conditional.* We do not pick and choose, obeying only when it is convenient or when doing so presents little or no challenge. On the contrary, we are "obedient from the heart." (Romans 6:17) We feel as did the Bible psalmist who wrote: "I shall show a fondness for your commandments that I have loved." (Psalm 119:47) Yes, we *love* to obey Jehovah. We recognize that he deserves—and requires—nothing less than our complete and unconditional obedience. (Deuteronomy 12:32) We want Jehovah to say of us what his Word says of Noah. Regarding that faithful patriarch, who showed love for God by being obedient over many decades, the Bible says: "Noah proceeded to do according to all that God had commanded him. He did just so."—Genesis 6:22.

¹² How does Jehovah feel about our willing obedience? His Word says that we thereby make his "heart rejoice." (Proverbs 27:11) Does our obedience really bring joy to the heart of the Sovereign Lord of the universe? Indeed, it does—and for good reason! Jehovah created us as free moral agents. This means that we have freedom of choice; we can choose to obey God, or we can choose to disobey him. (Deuteronomy 30:15, 16, 19, 20) When

---

* Even the wicked spirits can begrudgingly obey. When Jesus ordered the demons to come out of some possessed people, the demons were forced to recognize his authority and obey, although unwillingly.—Mark 1:27; 5:7-13.

---

12. When does our obedience bring joy to Jehovah's heart?

"This Is What the Love of God Means" 11

we willingly choose to obey Jehovah and when the motivating force behind that decision is a heart full of love for God, we bring great pleasure and joy to our heavenly Father. (Proverbs 11:20) We are also choosing the best way of life.

"HIS COMMANDMENTS ARE NOT BURDENSOME"

¹³ The apostle John tells us something very reassuring about Jehovah's requirements: "His commandments are not burdensome." The Greek word translated "burdensome" at 1 John 5:3 literally means "heavy."* Another Bible translation here reads: "His commandments do not weigh us down." (*New English Translation*) Jehovah's requirements are not unreasonable or oppressive. His laws are not beyond the ability of imperfect humans to obey.

¹⁴ We might illustrate it this way. A close friend asks you to help him move to another residence. There are many boxes to be transported. Some of them are light enough for one person to carry comfortably, but others are heavy and require two people to lift them. Your friend selects the boxes he wants you to move. Would he ask you to pick up boxes that he knows are too heavy for you? No. He would not want you to hurt yourself by trying to carry them alone. Similarly, our loving and kind God does not ask us to observe commandments

---

* At Matthew 23:4, this word is used to describe the *"heavy"* loads, the minute rules and man-made traditions that the scribes and Pharisees put upon the common people. The same word is rendered "oppressive" at Acts 20:29, 30 and refers to heavy-handed apostates who would "speak twisted things" and seek to mislead others.

13, 14. Why can it be said that God's "commandments are not burdensome," and how might this be illustrated?

that are too difficult to fulfill. (Deuteronomy 30:11-14) He would never ask us to carry such a heavy burden. Jehovah understands our limitations, for "he himself well knows the formation of us, remembering that we are dust."—Psalm 103:14.

[15] Jehovah's commandments are far from being burdensome; they are for our greatest good. (Isaiah 48:17) Moses could thus tell Israel of old: "Jehovah commanded us to carry out all these regulations, to fear Jehovah our God *for our good always,* that we might keep alive as at this day." (Deuteronomy 6:24) We too can be confident that in giving us his laws, Jehovah has our best interests at heart—our long-term, everlasting welfare. Really, how could it be otherwise? Jehovah is a God of infinite wisdom. (Romans 11:33) He therefore knows what is best for us. Jehovah is also the personification of love. (1 John 4:8) Love, his very essence, influences everything he says and does. It is the basis for all the commandments that he places upon his servants.

[16] This is not to say that obedience to God is an easy course to follow. We must fight against the influences of this debased world, which "is lying in the power of the wicked one." (1 John 5:19) We must also contend with the imperfect flesh, which inclines us toward violating God's laws. (Romans 7:21-25) But our love for God can win out. Jehovah blesses those who want to prove their love for him by their obedience. He gives his holy spirit "to those obeying him as ruler." (Acts 5:32) That spirit produces beautiful fruitage in us—precious qualities that

---

15. Why can we be confident that Jehovah's commandments are for our greatest good?
16. Despite the influences of this debased world and the tendencies of the imperfect flesh, why can we pursue an obedient course?

can aid us in pursuing an obedient course.—Galatians 5: 22, 23.

17 In this publication, we will examine Jehovah's principles and moral standards and many other indications of his will. As we do, we need to keep a number of important things in mind. Let us remember that Jehovah does not force us to obey his laws and principles; he wants willing obedience that stems from our heart. Let us not forget that Jehovah is asking us to live in a way that will bring rich blessings now and lead to everlasting life in the future. And let us see our wholehearted obedience for what it is—a precious opportunity to show Jehovah just how much we love him.

18 To help us discern right from wrong, Jehovah has lovingly endowed us with the faculty of conscience. Yet, to be a reliable guide, our conscience needs to be trained, as the next chapter will discuss.

17, 18. (a) What will we examine in this publication, and as we do, what should we keep in mind? (b) What will be discussed in the next chapter?

HOW WOULD YOU ANSWER?

- What kind of obedience does Jehovah expect from his worshippers, and why is this in our best interests?—Deuteronomy 5:28-33.
- How seriously does Jehovah take our obedience?—1 Samuel 15:22, 23.
- What lesson can we learn from Jesus' attitude toward obedience to God?—John 8:29.
- Why is it only right that we obey Jehovah? —Revelation 4:11.

CHAPTER 2

How Can You Maintain a Good Conscience?

"Hold a good conscience."
—1 PETER 3:16.

A MARINER steers his ship through the waves of a vast ocean; a hiker treks across a lonely wilderness; an aviator guides his aircraft as it soars above layers of clouds that stretch from one horizon to the other. Do you know what these individuals have in common? Each in his own way might be in big trouble without a compass—especially if other modern technology is not accessible.

[2] A compass is a simple instrument, usually just a dial with a magnetic needle that points northward. When it is working properly and especially when it is used in conjunction with an accurate map, it can be a lifesaver. In some ways, it may be likened to a precious gift that

1, 2. Why is a compass a vital instrument, and how may it be likened to the conscience?

Jehovah has given us—a conscience. (James 1:17) Without a conscience, we would be hopelessly lost. Used properly, it can help us find our way and keep to the right path in life. So let us consider what the conscience is and how it works. Then we can discuss these points: (1) How the conscience may be trained, (2) why we should consider the consciences of others, and (3) how a good conscience brings blessings.

WHAT THE CONSCIENCE IS AND HOW IT WORKS

³ In the Bible, the Greek word for "conscience" literally means "co-knowledge, or knowledge with oneself." Unlike all other earthly creatures, we possess a God-given capacity to know ourselves. We can, in a sense, stand back and look at ourselves and make moral judgments. Acting as an internal witness bearer, or judge, our conscience can examine our actions, our attitudes, and our choices. It may guide us toward a good decision or warn us against a bad one. Afterward, it may comfort us for choosing well or punish us with sharp pangs for choosing poorly.

⁴ This faculty was built into man and woman from the very beginning. Adam and Eve each showed that they had a conscience. We see evidence to that effect in the shame they experienced following their sin. (Genesis 3: 7, 8) Sadly, a troubled conscience could do them no good by then. They had deliberately ignored God's law. Thus they knowingly chose to become rebels, opponents of

---

3. What is the literal meaning of the Greek word for "conscience," and what unique capacity in humans does it describe?
4, 5. (a) How do we know that Adam and Eve each had a conscience, and what resulted because they ignored God's law? (b) What examples show the conscience at work in faithful men of pre-Christian times?

Jehovah God. As perfect humans, they knew what they were doing, and there was no turning back.

⁵ Unlike Adam and Eve, many imperfect humans have heeded their conscience. For example, the faithful man Job was able to say: "On my justness I have laid hold, and I shall not let it go; my heart will not taunt me for any of my days."* (Job 27:6) Job was truly a conscientious man. He was careful to listen to his conscience, letting it guide his actions and decisions. Thus, he could say with real satisfaction that his conscience did not taunt him, or torment him, with shame and guilt. Notice the contrast between Job and David. When David showed disrespect for Saul, Jehovah's anointed king, "it came about afterward that David's heart kept striking him." (1 Samuel 24:5) Those sharp pangs of conscience surely benefited David, teaching him to avoid such disrespect thereafter.

⁶ Does this gift of conscience belong exclusively to servants of Jehovah? Consider the apostle Paul's inspired words: "Whenever people of the nations that do not have law do by nature the things of the law, these people, although not having law, are a law to themselves. They are the very ones who demonstrate the matter of the law to be written in their hearts, while their conscience is bearing witness with them and, between their own thoughts, they are being accused or even excused."

---

* No specific word for "conscience" appears in the Hebrew Scriptures. However, the conscience is clearly in evidence in such examples as this one. The expression "heart" generally refers to the inner person. In such instances as this, it evidently points to a specific part of the inner man—his conscience. In the Christian Greek Scriptures, the Greek word rendered "conscience" occurs some 30 times.

---

6. What shows that conscience is a gift to all mankind?

(Romans 2:14, 15) Even those who are completely unfamiliar with Jehovah's laws may at times be moved by this internal witness to act in harmony with divine principles.

[7] However, the conscience may in some cases be wrong. Why? Well, if a compass is placed near a metal object, it may be influenced to point in a direction other than north. And if it is used without an accurate map, the compass may be nearly worthless. Similarly, if unduly influenced by the selfish desires of our heart, our conscience may point us in the wrong direction. And if it is used without the sure guidance of God's Word, we may be unable to distinguish between right and wrong in many important matters. Really, in order for our conscience to work properly, we need the guidance of Jehovah's holy spirit. Paul wrote: "My conscience bears witness with me in holy spirit." (Romans 9:1) How, though, can we make sure that our conscience is in harmony with Jehovah's holy spirit? It is a matter of training.

HOW THE CONSCIENCE MAY BE TRAINED

[8] How do you make a decision that is based on conscience? Some, it seems, simply look within, examine their feelings, and decide what to do. They may then say, "Well, it doesn't bother my conscience." The desires of the heart can be very strong, even swaying the conscience. The Bible says: "The heart is more treacherous than anything else and is desperate. Who can know it?" (Jeremiah 17:9) What our heart desires, then, should not

---

7. Why may the conscience be wrong at times?
8. (a) How may the heart affect the conscience, and what should matter most in our decisions? (b) Why is a clear conscience not always sufficient for a Christian? (See footnote.)

be the most important consideration. Rather, we want to consider first what will please Jehovah God.*

9 If a decision is truly based on our trained conscience, it will reflect our godly fear, not our personal desires. Consider a case in point. The faithful governor Nehemiah had a right to exact certain payments and dues from the people in Jerusalem. Yet, he held back. Why? He hated the very thought of risking Jehovah's displeasure by oppressing God's people. He said: "I did not do that way on account of the fear of God." (Nehemiah 5:15) Sincere godly fear, a wholehearted fear of displeasing our heavenly Father, is essential. Such reverential fear will move us to seek direction from God's Word when we have decisions to make.

10 For instance, consider the matter of alcoholic beverages. Here is a decision that many of us face in social settings, Will I drink or not? First, we need to educate ourselves. What Bible principles bear on the matter? Well, the Bible does not condemn the moderate use of alcohol. It praises Jehovah for the gift of wine. (Psalm 104:14, 15) However, the Bible condemns heavy drinking and revelries. (Luke 21:34; Romans 13:13) Moreover, it lists drunk-

---

* The Bible shows that having a *clear* conscience is not always sufficient. For example, Paul said: "I am not conscious of anything against myself. Yet by this I am not proved righteous, but he that examines me is Jehovah." (1 Corinthians 4:4) Even those who persecute Christians, as Paul once did, may do so with a clear conscience because they think that God approves of their course. It is vital that our conscience be both clear in our eyes and clean in God's eyes. —Acts 23:1; 2 Timothy 1:3.

9. What is godly fear, and how may our having it affect our conscience?
10, 11. What Bible principles bear on the matter of drinking alcoholic beverages, and how may we get God's guidance in applying them?

enness among other very serious sins, such as fornication and adultery.*—1 Corinthians 6:9, 10.

[11] A Christian's conscience is educated and sensitized by such principles. So when we face a decision about drinking at a gathering, we ask ourselves such questions as these: 'What kind of gathering is being organized? Is it likely to get out of hand, becoming a revelry? What are my own tendencies? Do I long for alcohol, depend on it, use it to control my moods and behavior? Do I have the self-control needed to limit my drinking?' As we ponder Bible principles and the questions they evoke, we do well to pray for Jehovah's guidance. (Psalm 139:23, 24) In this way, we are inviting Jehovah to guide us with his holy spirit. We are also training our conscience to be in tune with divine principles. There is another factor, though, that should weigh in our decisions.

WHY CONSIDER THE CONSCIENCES OF OTHERS?

[12] You may find yourself surprised at times by the degree to which Christian consciences differ. One person finds a practice or custom objectionable; another enjoys it and sees no basis for condemning it. In the matter of social drinking, for example, one finds delight in taking a drink with a few friends as they relax together for an evening; another is troubled by the practice. Why are there such differences, and how should they affect our decisions?

[13] People differ for many reasons. Backgrounds vary greatly. Some, for instance, are acutely aware of a

---

* It should be noted that many doctors say that controlled drinking is not really possible for alcoholics; for them, "moderation" means not drinking.

12, 13. What are some reasons why Christian consciences differ, and how should we deal with such differences?

weakness that they have struggled with in the past—perhaps not always successfully. (1 Kings 8:38, 39) When it comes to alcohol, such individuals would likely feel particularly sensitive. If such a person comes to your home for a visit, his conscience may rightly move him to refuse the offer of a drink. Will you be offended? Will you insist? No. Whether you know his reasons or not—reasons that he may choose to keep private in this setting—brotherly love will move you to be considerate.

[14] The apostle Paul saw that consciences often varied widely among Christians in the first century. Back then, some Christians were troubled about certain foods that had been sacrificed to idols. (1 Corinthians 10:25) Paul's conscience did not object to such foods that were subsequently sold at markets. To him, idols were nothing; idols could never own food that originated with Jehovah and belonged to Him anyway. Yet, Paul understood that others did not share his view of this matter. Some might have been deeply involved with idolatry before becoming Christians. To them, anything even formerly connected with idolatry was offensive. The solution?

[15] Paul said: "We, though, who are strong ought to bear the weaknesses of those not strong, and not to be pleasing ourselves. For even the Christ did not please himself." (Romans 15:1, 3) Paul reasoned that we should put the needs of our brothers ahead of our own, just as Christ did. In a related discussion, Paul said that he would rather not eat meat at all than stumble a precious sheep for whom Christ had given his life.—1 Corinthians 8:13; 10:23, 24, 31-33.

[16] On the other hand, those with a more restrictive

14, 15. Over what issue did the consciences of those in the first-century congregation differ, and what did Paul recommend?
16. Why should those with a more restrictive conscience avoid judging those whose conscience differs from theirs?

A Bible-trained conscience can help you to decide whether to drink alcoholic beverages or not

conscience should not be critical of others, insisting that all view matters of conscience just as they do. (Romans 14:10) Really, the conscience is best used as an internal judge, not as a license to judge others. Remember Jesus' words: "Stop judging that you may not be judged." (Matthew 7:1) All in the congregation want to avoid making an issue of personal matters of conscience. Instead, we seek ways to promote love and unity, building one another up, not tearing one another down.—Romans 14:19.

HOW A GOOD CONSCIENCE BRINGS BLESSINGS

[17] The apostle Peter wrote: "Hold a good conscience." (1 Peter 3:16) A conscience that is clean in the sight of

---

17. What has happened to the consciences of many today?

A good conscience can guide us on life's journey, bringing joy and inner peace

Jehovah God is a tremendous blessing. It is not like the consciences of so many today. Paul described those who are "marked in their conscience as with a branding iron." (1 Timothy 4:2) A branding iron sears the flesh, leaving it scarred and insensitive. Many have a conscience that is, in effect, dead—so scarred and insensitive that it no longer sends out warnings, protests, or pangs of shame or guilt over wrongdoing. "Good riddance," many today seem to say to such feelings as guilt.

¹⁸ In truth, feelings of guilt can be the conscience's way of telling us that we have done wrong. When such

---

18, 19. (a) Feelings of guilt or shame may have what value? (b) What can we do if our conscience continues to punish us for past sins for which we have already repented?

feelings move a sinner to repent, even the worst of sins may be forgiven. King David, for example, became guilty of grave wrongdoing but was forgiven largely because of his sincere repentance. His hatred of his wrong course and his determination to obey Jehovah's laws from then on led him to see firsthand that Jehovah is "good and ready to forgive." (Psalm 51:1-19; 86:5) What, though, if intense feelings of guilt and shame persist after we have repented and have received forgiveness?

[19] Sometimes the conscience can be overly punitive, beating a sinner with guilt long after such feelings stop serving any useful purpose. In such cases, we may need to assure the self-condemning heart that Jehovah is greater than all human feelings. We need to believe in and accept his love and forgiveness, just as we encourage others to do. (1 John 3:19, 20) On the other hand, a cleansed conscience brings inner peace, serenity, and a profound joy that is rarely found in this world. Many who were once involved in serious sin have experienced this marvelous relief and are able today to hold a good conscience as they serve Jehovah God.—1 Corinthians 6:11.

[20] This book is designed to help you find that joy, to hold a good conscience throughout the rest of these troubled last days of Satan's system of things. Of course, it cannot cover all of the Bible's laws and principles that you need to think about and apply in the situations that arise day by day. Furthermore, do not expect simple, black-and-white rules on matters of conscience. The purpose of this book is to help you educate and sensitize

---

20, 21. (a) What is this publication designed to help you to do? (b) As Christians, we enjoy what freedom, yet how should we use it?

your conscience by studying how to apply God's Word in your daily life. Unlike the Mosaic Law, "the law of the Christ" invites its adherents to live more by conscience and principle than by written rules. (Galatians 6:2) Jehovah thus entrusts Christians with extraordinary freedom. However, his Word reminds us never to use that freedom as "a blind for badness." (1 Peter 2:16) Rather, such freedom affords us a marvelous opportunity to express our love for Jehovah.

21 By prayerfully considering how best to live by Bible principles and then putting your decisions to work, you will continue a vital process that began when you first came to know Jehovah. Your "perceptive powers" will be trained "through use." (Hebrews 5:14) Your Bible-trained conscience will be a blessing to you every day of your life. Like the compass that guides the traveler, your conscience will help you to make decisions that please your heavenly Father. This is a sure way to keep yourself in God's love.

HOW WOULD YOU ANSWER?

- How should our conscience be influenced by the knowledge that Jehovah is watching over us at all times?—Hebrews 4:13.
- How did Joseph's conscience help him to resist temptation?—Genesis 39:1, 2, 7-12.
- Why is a clean conscience essential in order to approach Jehovah?—Hebrews 10:22.
- Why should we be concerned about the consciences of unbelievers?—2 Corinthians 4:1, 2.

CHAPTER 3

Love Those Whom God Loves

"He that is walking with wise persons will become wise."—PROVERBS 13:20.

IN A way, people are like sponges; they tend to absorb whatever surrounds them. It is all too easy to adopt —even unwittingly—the attitudes, standards, and personality traits of those with whom we have close association.

² The Bible expresses an inescapable truth when it says: "He that is walking with wise persons will become wise, but he that is having dealings with the stupid ones will fare badly." (Proverbs 13:20) This proverb speaks about more than casual contact. The expression "walking with" suggests ongoing association.* Commenting on this verse, one Bible reference work says: "To walk with a person implies love and attachment." Would you not agree that we tend to imitate those we love? Indeed, because we attach ourselves emotionally to those we love, they can have a molding effect on us—for good or for bad.

³ To remain in God's love, it is vital that we seek out associates who will influence us for the good. How can we do that? Put simply, we can do so by loving those

---

* The Hebrew word rendered "have dealings with" is also rendered "to associate" and "have companionship."—Judges 14:20; Proverbs 22:24.

1-3. (a) What inescapable truth does the Bible express? (b) How can we choose associates who will influence us for the good?

whom God loves, making his friends our friends. Think about it. What better associates could we choose than those who have the qualities that Jehovah looks for in his friends? Let us, then, examine the kind of people who are loved by God. With Jehovah's viewpoint clearly in mind, we will be better equipped to choose wholesome associates.

THOSE WHOM GOD LOVES

⁴ When it comes to friendship, Jehovah is particular. Does he not have the right to be? After all, he is the Sovereign Lord of the universe, and friendship with him is the greatest of all privileges. Whom, then, does he choose as his friends? Jehovah draws close to those who trust in him and put their full faith in him. Consider, for example, the patriarch Abraham, a man known for his outstanding faith. It is hard to imagine a greater test of faith for a human father than to be asked to offer up his son as a sacrifice.* Yet, Abraham "as good as offered up Isaac," having full faith "that God was able to raise him up even from the dead." (Hebrews 11:17-19) Because Abraham displayed such faith and obedience, Jehovah affectionately referred to him as "my friend." —Isaiah 41:8; James 2:21-23.

⁵ Jehovah places a high value on loyal obedience. He loves those who are willing to put loyalty to him above all else. (2 Samuel 22:26) As we saw in Chapter 1 of this

---

* By asking this of Abraham, Jehovah provided a glimpse of the sacrifice he himself would make in offering up his only-begotten Son. (John 3:16) In Abraham's case, Jehovah intervened and provided a ram as a substitute for Isaac.—Genesis 22:1, 2, 9-13.

4. Why does Jehovah have the right to be particular about his friends, and why did Jehovah refer to Abraham as "my friend"?
5. How does Jehovah view those who loyally obey him?

publication, Jehovah finds great pleasure in those who choose to obey him out of love. "His intimacy," says Proverbs 3:32, "is with the upright ones." Those who loyally meet God's requirements receive a gracious invitation from Jehovah: They can be guests in his "tent" —welcomed to worship him and granted free access to him in prayer.—Psalm 15:1-5.

⁶ Jehovah loves those who love Jesus, his only-begotten Son. Jesus said: "If anyone loves me, he will observe my word, and my Father will love him, and we shall come to him and make our abode with him." (John 14:23) How can we show our love for Jesus? Surely by observing his commandments, including the commission to preach the good news and make disciples. (Matthew 28:19, 20; John 14:15, 21) We also show our love for Jesus when we "follow his steps closely," imitating him in word and deed to the best of our ability as imperfect humans. (1 Peter 2:21) Jehovah's heart is touched by the efforts of those whose love for his Son moves them to pursue a Christlike course.

⁷ Faith, loyalty, obedience, and love for Jesus and his ways—these are among the qualities that Jehovah looks for in His friends. Each of us does well to ask himself: 'Are such qualities and ways evident in my close associates? Have I made Jehovah's friends my friends?' It is wise to do so. Individuals who cultivate godly qualities and preach the Kingdom good news with zeal can have a positive effect on us, influencing us to live up to our determination to please God.—See the box "What Is a Good Friend?" on page 29.

---

6. How can we show that we love Jesus, and how does Jehovah feel about those who love his Son?
7. Why is it wise to befriend Jehovah's friends?

LEARNING FROM A BIBLE EXAMPLE

⁸ The Scriptures contain many examples of those who benefited as a result of choosing wholesome associates. You can read about the relationship between Naomi and her daughter-in-law Ruth, between the three young Hebrews who stuck together in Babylon, and between Paul and Timothy. (Ruth 1:16; Daniel 3:17, 18; 1 Corinthians 4:17; Philippians 2:20-22) Let us, though, focus on another outstanding example: the friendship between David and Jonathan.

⁹ The Bible says that after David slew Goliath, "Jonathan's very soul became bound up with the soul of David, and Jonathan began to love him as his own soul." (1 Samuel 18:1) Thus began an unbreakable friendship that despite a significant age difference, persisted until Jonathan's death on the battlefield.* (2 Samuel 1:26) What was the basis of the strong bond forged between these two friends?

¹⁰ David and Jonathan were bound together by their love for God and their strong desire to remain faithful to him. These two men shared a spiritual bond. Each displayed qualities that endeared him to the other. Jonathan no doubt was impressed with the courage and zeal of the young man who fearlessly defended Jehovah's name. David undoubtedly respected the older

---

* David was a youth—"but a boy"—when he felled Goliath and was about 30 at the time of Jonathan's death. (1 Samuel 17:33; 31:2; 2 Samuel 5:4) Jonathan, who was about 60 when he died, was evidently some 30 years older than David.

---

8. What impresses you about the relationship between (a) Naomi and Ruth? (b) the three young Hebrews? (c) Paul and Timothy?
9, 10. What was the basis of the friendship between David and Jonathan?

man who loyally supported Jehovah's arrangements and unselfishly put David's interests ahead of his own. Consider, for example, what happened when David was at a low point in his life, living as a fugitive in the wilderness to escape the wrath of wicked King Saul, Jonathan's father. In a remarkable demonstration of loyalty, Jonathan took the initiative and "went to David . . . that he might

WHAT IS A GOOD FRIEND?

Principle: "A true companion is loving all the time, and is a brother that is born for when there is distress."—Proverbs 17:17.

Some questions to ask yourself

- Are my friends also friends of Jehovah and Jesus?—John 15:14, 16; James 2:23.

- Do my friends help me to develop good habits? —1 Corinthians 15:33.

- Do my friends love me enough to correct me if necessary?—Psalm 141:5; Proverbs 27:6.

- What do my speech and actions reveal about the type of friend I am to others?—Proverbs 12:18; 18:24; 1 John 3:16-18.

> ## HOW WE MADE GOOD FRIENDS
>
> - "At first, I found it difficult to make friends in the congregation. But I discovered that having an active share in the ministry helped me to develop such qualities as patience, endurance, and self-sacrificing love. As I continue to develop these qualities, I find that like-minded people are attracted to me, and I now have some good friends."—Shivani.
>
> - "I prayed that I could find friends inside the congregation. But for a long time, I felt that my prayers were not being answered. I eventually realized that I wasn't really doing anything to make friends. I wasn't taking the initiative. Since I began acting in harmony with my prayers, however, I definitely feel that Jehovah has answered them."—Ryan.

strengthen his hand in regard to God." (1 Samuel 23:16) Imagine how David must have felt when his dear friend came and offered him support and encouragement!*

¹¹ What do we learn from the example of Jonathan and David? Above all, we see that the most important thing for friends to have in common is spiritual values. When we draw close to those who share our beliefs, our

---

* As recorded at 1 Samuel 23:17, Jonathan said five things to encourage David: (1) He urged David not to be afraid. (2) He assured David that Saul's efforts would fail. (3) He reminded David that he would receive the kingship, as God had promised. (4) He pledged his loyalty to David. (5) He told David that even Saul was aware of Jonathan's loyalty to David.

11. What do you learn about friendship from the example of Jonathan and David?

moral values, and our desire to remain faithful to God, there can be an interchange of thoughts, feelings, and experiences that encourage and upbuild us. (Romans 1: 11, 12) We find such spiritually-minded associates among fellow worshippers. Does this mean, though, that everyone who comes to meetings at the Kingdom Hall is a good associate? No, not necessarily.

CHOOSING OUR CLOSE ASSOCIATES

[12] Even within the congregation, we must be selective if our associates are to be spiritually upbuilding. Should this surprise us? Not really. Some Christians in the congregation may take longer to reach spiritual maturity, even as some fruit on a tree may take longer to ripen. Thus, in any given congregation, we find Christians who are at different levels of spiritual growth. (Hebrews 5:12–6:3) Of course, we show patience and love to newer or weaker ones, for we want to help them to grow spiritually.—Romans 14:1; 15:1.

[13] Occasionally, there may be a situation in the congregation that calls for us to watch our association. Some individuals might engage in questionable conduct. Others may develop a bitter or complaining spirit. Congregations in the first century C.E. faced a similar challenge. While most members were faithful, some individuals did not conduct themselves aright. Because some in the congregation in Corinth did not uphold certain Christian teachings, the apostle Paul warned the congregation: "Do not be misled. Bad associations spoil useful habits." (1 Corinthians 15:12, 33) Paul cautioned Timothy that even among fellow Christians, there might be

---

12, 13. (a) Why must we be selective in choosing associates even from among fellow Christians? (b) What challenge did first-century congregations face, prompting Paul to give what strong warnings?

some who do not act honorably. Timothy was told to keep clear of such ones, not making them his close associates.—2 Timothy 2:20-22.

¹⁴ How can we apply the principle behind Paul's warnings? By avoiding close association with anyone—inside or outside the congregation—who could be a corrupting influence. (2 Thessalonians 3:6, 7, 14) We must protect our spirituality. Remember that like a sponge, we absorb the attitudes and ways of our close friends. Just as we cannot submerge a sponge in vinegar and expect it to fill with water, so we cannot associate with those who exert a negative influence and expect to absorb what is positive.—1 Corinthians 5:6.

¹⁵ Thankfully, the potential for finding wholesome associates among fellow worshippers is great indeed. (Psalm 133:1) How can you find spiritually-minded friends in the congregation? As you cultivate godly qualities and ways, no doubt others of like mind will be drawn to you. At the same time, you may need to take some practical steps to reach out and make new friends. (See the box "How We Made Good Friends," on page 30.) Look for those who display the qualities you want to reflect. Heed the Bible's counsel to "widen out," seeking out friendships with fellow believers regardless of race, nationality, or culture. (2 Corinthians 6:13; 1 Peter 2:17) Do not limit yourself to those of your own age group. Remember that Jonathan was much older than David. Many older ones can bring to friendship a rich supply of experience and wisdom.

---

14. How can we apply the principle behind Paul's warnings about associations?
15. What can you do to find spiritually-minded friends in the congregation?

You can find wholesome associates among fellow worshippers

WHEN DIFFICULTIES ARISE

¹⁶ Since there is a wide variety of personalities and backgrounds in the congregation, problems may arise from time to time. A fellow believer might say or do something that hurts our feelings. (Proverbs 12:18) Sometimes difficulties are fueled by personality clashes, misunderstandings, or differences of opinion. Will we stumble over such challenges and keep away from the congregation? Not if we have genuine love for Jehovah and for those whom he loves.

¹⁷ As our Creator and Life-Sustainer, Jehovah deserves our love and complete devotion. (Revelation 4:11) In addition, the congregation that he is pleased to use

---

16, 17. If a fellow worshipper hurts us in some way, why should we not withdraw from the congregation?

deserves our loyal support. (Hebrews 13:17) So if a fellow worshipper hurts us or disappoints us in some way, we will not withdraw from the congregation as a means of protest. How could we? Jehovah is not the one who offended us. Our love for Jehovah could never allow us to turn our back on him and his people!—Psalm 119:165.

[18] Love for fellow worshippers moves us to promote peace in the congregation. Jehovah does not expect perfection from those he loves, and neither should we. Love enables us to overlook minor trespasses, remembering that we are all imperfect and make mistakes. (Proverbs 17:9; 1 Peter 4:8) Love helps us to continue "forgiving one another freely." (Colossians 3:13) It is not always easy to apply this counsel. If we allow negative emotions to get the better of us, we may be inclined to hold on to resentment, perhaps feeling that our anger is somehow punishing the offender. In reality, though, holding on to resentment is harmful to us. Choosing to forgive when there is a sound basis for doing so brings rich blessings. (Luke 17:3, 4) It gives us peace of mind and heart, preserves peace in the congregation and, above all, safeguards our relationship with Jehovah.—Matthew 6:14, 15; Romans 14:19.

WHEN TO WITHDRAW FELLOWSHIP

[19] At times, we are called upon to withdraw our fellowship from one who has been a member of the congregation. This situation arises when an individual who unrepentantly violates God's law is disfellowshipped or

---

18. (a) What can we do to promote peace in the congregation? (b) Choosing to forgive when there is a sound basis for doing so brings what blessings?
19. What situations may arise that make it necessary for us to withdraw our fellowship from someone?

when one rejects the faith by teaching false doctrine or by disassociating himself from the congregation. God's Word plainly tells us to "quit mixing in company" with such ones.* (1 Corinthians 5:11-13; 2 John 9-11) It may be a real challenge to avoid someone who had perhaps been a friend or who is related to us. Will we take a firm stand, thereby showing that we put loyalty to Jehovah and his righteous laws above all else? Remember that Jehovah places a high value on loyalty and obedience.

20 The disfellowshipping arrangement is really a loving provision from Jehovah. How so? Expelling an unrepentant sinner shows love for Jehovah's holy name and all that it stands for. (1 Peter 1:15, 16) Disfellowshipping keeps the congregation safe. Faithful members are protected from the unwholesome influence of willful sinners and can go about their worship knowing that the congregation is a safe haven from this wicked world. (1 Corinthians 5:7; Hebrews 12:15, 16) The strong discipline shows love for the wrongdoer. It may be just the jolt he needs to come to his senses and take the steps necessary to return to Jehovah.—Hebrews 12:11.

21 We cannot escape the fact that our close associates can have a powerful, molding effect on us. It is vital, then, that we choose our associates wisely. By making Jehovah's friends our friends, by loving those whom God loves, we will surround ourselves with the best possible associates. What we absorb from them will help us to live up to our determination to please Jehovah.

---

* For more information on how to treat disfellowshipped or disassociated ones, see the Appendix, pages 207-9.

20, 21. (a) Why is the disfellowshipping arrangement a loving one? (b) Why is it vital that we choose our associates wisely?

CHAPTER 4

Why Respect Authority?

"Honor men of all sorts."
—1 PETER 2:17.

HAVE you ever watched a small child react when he is asked to do something he really does not want to do? You may see quite a conflict written plainly on that little boy's face. He hears his parent's voice, and he knows that he is supposed to respect his parent's authority. But in this case, he just does not *want* to obey. His struggle illustrates a truth we all face.

² Respect for authority does not always come easily to us. Do you sometimes find it difficult to respect those who have a measure of authority over you? If so, you are not alone in this struggle. We live at a time when respect for authority seems to be at an all-time low. Yet, the Bible says that we need to show respect for those who hold positions of authority over us. (Proverbs 24:21) In fact, doing so is essential if we want to remain in God's love. Naturally, then, some questions arise. Why can it be so difficult for us to respect authority? Why does Jehovah ask this of us, and what will help us to comply? Finally, in what ways can we show respect for authority?

WHY IT IS A CHALLENGE

³ Let us briefly consider two reasons why it can be such a challenge for us to show respect for those in authori-

---
1, 2. (a) What struggle do we face when it comes to authority? (b) What questions will we consider?
3, 4. How did sin and imperfection begin, and why does our sinful nature make it a challenge for us to respect authority?

ty. First, imperfection afflicts us; second, it afflicts those humans in authority over us. Human sin and imperfection got their start a long time ago, back in the garden of Eden when Adam and Eve rebelled against God's authority. So sin began with rebellion. To this day, we have an inborn tendency to rebel.—Genesis 2:15-17; 3:1-7; Psalm 51:5; Romans 5:12.

[4] Because of our sinful nature, pride and haughtiness arise easily in most of us, whereas humility is a rare quality that we need to work hard to cultivate and maintain. Even after years of faithful service to God, we may give in to stubbornness and pride. For example, consider Korah, who faithfully stuck with Jehovah's people through many hardships. Still, he craved more authority and brazenly led a rebellion against Moses, the meekest man alive at that time. (Numbers 12:3; 16:1-3) Think, too, of King Uzziah, whose pride led him to enter Jehovah's temple and carry out a sacred duty reserved for the priests. (2 Chronicles 26:16-21) Such men paid dearly for their rebellion. Yet, their negative examples are useful reminders for all of us. We need to combat the pride that makes it difficult for us to respect authority.

[5] On the other hand, imperfect humans in positions of power have done much to undermine respect for authority. Many have been cruel, abusive, or tyrannical. In fact, human history is largely a record of the abuse of power. (Ecclesiastes 8:9) For example, Saul was a good, humble man when Jehovah chose him to be king. However, he succumbed to pride and jealousy; he then persecuted the faithful man David. (1 Samuel 9:20, 21; 10:20-22; 18:7-11) David later became one of the best kings Israel ever had, yet he misused his power when he stole the wife of

---

5. How have imperfect humans misused their authority?

Uriah the Hittite and sent that innocent man to the front lines to be killed in battle. (2 Samuel 11:1-17) Yes, imperfection makes it hard for people to handle power well. And when those in power do not respect Jehovah, they do even worse. After describing the way that some Catholic popes instituted widespread persecution, a British statesman wrote: "Power tends to corrupt, and absolute power corrupts absolutely." With such a record in mind, let us consider the question: Why should we respect authority?

WHY RESPECT AUTHORITY?

[6] The best reasons to respect authority spring from love—our love for Jehovah, for our fellow man, and even for ourselves. Because we love Jehovah above all else, we want to make his heart rejoice. (Proverbs 27:11; Mark 12:29, 30) We know that his sovereignty, his right to rule the universe, has been challenged on earth ever since the rebellion in Eden and that the majority of mankind have sided with Satan and rejected Jehovah's rule. We are thrilled to take the opposite stand. When we read the majestic words of Revelation 4:11, they strike a chord in our heart. How clear it is to us that Jehovah is the rightful Ruler of the universe! We embrace Jehovah's sovereignty, accepting his rule in our day-to-day life.

[7] Such respect means obedience and more. We obey Jehovah readily because we love him. However, there are bound to be times when obedience will be very difficult for us. At such times we, like that little boy described at the outset, will need to learn submission. We recall that Jesus submitted to his Father's will even when doing so could seem very challenging. "Let, not my will, but yours take place," he said to his Father.—Luke 22:42.

6, 7. (a) What does our love for Jehovah move us to do, and why? (b) What attitude does submission involve, and how may we show it?

⁸ Of course, Jehovah does not speak to us individually today; he uses his Word and human representatives on earth. Most often, then, we show submission to Jehovah's authority by respecting those humans he has placed, or has allowed to continue, in positions of authority over us. If we were to rebel against those humans —for example, by refusing to accept their Scriptural counsel and correction—we would offend our God. When the Israelites murmured and rebelled against Moses, Jehovah took their actions personally as directed against him. —Numbers 14:26, 27.

⁹ We also show respect for authority out of love for our fellow man. How so? Well, imagine that you are a soldier in an army. The success, even the very survival of the army, likely depends on each soldier's cooperation with, obedience to, and respect for the chain of command. If you were to undermine that organization by rebelling, all your fellow soldiers might well be placed in danger. Granted, human armies wreak terrible havoc in the world today. However, Jehovah has armies that do only good. The Bible refers to God hundreds of times as "Jehovah of armies." (1 Samuel 1:3) He is the Commander of a vast array of mighty spirit creatures. At times, Jehovah likens his earthly servants to an army. (Psalm 68:11; Ezekiel 37:1-10) If we were to rebel against the humans that Jehovah has put in authority over us, might we not be putting our fellow spiritual soldiers at risk? When a Christian rebels against appointed elders, others in the

---

8. (a) Submission to Jehovah's authority today often involves what, and what reveals Jehovah's feelings in this regard? (b) What can help us to listen to counsel and accept discipline? (See the box on pages 46-7.)
9. Why will our love for our fellow man move us to respect authority? Illustrate.

A Christian father imitates the way Christ handles headship

congregation may suffer as well. (1 Corinthians 12:14, 25, 26) When a child rebels, the whole family may suffer. So we show our love for our fellow man by developing a respectful and cooperative spirit.

¹⁰ We also respect authority because it is in our own best interests to do so. When Jehovah asks us to respect authority, he often mentions the benefits that will come to us for doing so. For instance, he tells children to obey their parents in order to live a long and good life. (Deuteronomy 5:16; Ephesians 6:2, 3) He tells us to respect congregation elders because failure to do so will cause us spiritual harm. (Hebrews 13:7, 17) And he tells us to obey secular authorities for our own protection.—Romans 13:4.

¹¹ Would you not agree that knowing why Jehovah wants us to obey helps us to respect authority? Let us,

---

10, 11. How does a proper desire to benefit ourselves move us to be obedient to authority?

RESPECT IN THE FAMILY

[12] Jehovah himself designed the family arrangement. Ever the God of order, he has organized the family so that it can work well. (1 Corinthians 14:33) He gives the husband and father authority to act as family head. The husband shows respect for his Head, Christ Jesus, by imitating the way Jesus exercises headship over the congregation. (Ephesians 5:23) Thus, the husband is not to abdicate his responsibility but to shoulder it manfully; nor is he to be tyrannical or harsh but, rather, loving, reasonable, and kind. He keeps in mind that his authority is relative—it never overrules Jehovah's authority.

[13] A wife and mother is to act as her husband's helper, or complement. She too is vested with authority in the family, for the Bible speaks of "the law of your mother." (Proverbs 1:8) Of course, her authority is subordinate to that of her husband. A Christian wife shows respect for her husband's authority by

---

12. What role does Jehovah assign to the husband and father in the family, and how may a man fulfill that role?
13. How may a wife and mother fulfill her family role in a way that pleases Jehovah?

> ## WHOSE AUTHORITY SHOULD I OBEY?
>
> **Principle:** "Jehovah is our Judge, Jehovah is our Statute-giver, Jehovah is our King."—Isaiah 33:22.
>
> ### Some questions to ask yourself
>
> - What would I do if I were asked to violate Jehovah's standards?—Matthew 22:37-39; 26:52; John 18:36.
>
> - What would I do if I were ordered to refrain from carrying out Jehovah's commands?—Acts 5:27-29; Hebrews 10:24, 25.
>
> - What can help me to want to obey those in positions of authority?—Romans 13:1-4; 1 Corinthians 11:3; Ephesians 6:1-3.

helping him fulfill his role as family head. She does not belittle him, manipulate him, or usurp his position. Rather, she is supportive and cooperative. When his decisions are not to her liking, she may respectfully express her thoughts, but she remains submissive. If her husband is not a believer, she may face challenging situations, yet her submissive conduct may move her husband to seek Jehovah.—1 Peter 3:1.

[14] Children bring delight to Jehovah's heart when they obey their father and mother. They also bring honor and joy to their parents. (Proverbs 10:1) In single-parent families, children apply the same principle of obedience, aware that their parent may have an even greater need for their support and cooperation. In families where all members fulfill the roles that God designed for them, a great deal of peace and joy results. This reflects well on

---

14. How may children bring joy to their parents and to Jehovah?

the Originator of all families, Jehovah God.—Ephesians 3:14, 15.

RESPECT IN THE CONGREGATION

15 Jehovah has appointed his Son as Ruler over the Christian congregation. (Colossians 1:13) Jesus, in turn, has assigned his "faithful and discreet slave" to look after the spiritual needs of God's people on earth. (Matthew 24:45-47) The Governing Body of Jehovah's Witnesses represents the slave class. As in the first-century Christian congregations, elders today receive instructions and counsel from the Governing Body, either directly or through its representatives, such as traveling overseers. When we as individuals respect the authority of Christian elders, we are obeying Jehovah.—Hebrews 13:17.

16 Elders and ministerial servants are not perfect. They have failings, as we do. Yet, the elders are "gifts in men," provided to help the congregation remain spiritually strong. (Ephesians 4:8) Elders are appointed by holy spirit. (Acts 20:28) How so? In that such men must first meet the qualifications recorded in God's spirit-inspired Word. (1 Timothy 3:1-7, 12; Titus 1:5-9) Further, the elders who evaluate a brother's qualifications pray earnestly for the guidance of Jehovah's holy spirit.

17 In the congregation, there may be times when no elders and ministerial servants are available to perform a task normally assigned to them, such as conducting a meeting for field service. In such instances, other

---

15. (a) How may we show in the congregation that we respect Jehovah's authority? (b) What principles may help us to be obedient to those taking the lead? (See the box on pages 48-9.)
16. In what sense are elders appointed by holy spirit?
17. In their congregation activity, why do Christian women at times wear head coverings?

baptized brothers may fill in. If none are available, then qualified Christian sisters may fill such needs. However, when a woman fills a role normally assigned to a baptized male, she wears a head covering.* (1 Corinthians 11:3-10) This requirement does not demean women. Rather, it provides an opportunity to show respect for Jehovah's arrangement of headship, both in the family and in the congregation.

RESPECT FOR SECULAR AUTHORITY

[18] True Christians conscientiously adhere to the principles stated at Romans 13:1-7. As you read over that passage, you can see that "the superior authorities" mentioned there are the secular governments. As long as Jehovah allows these human powers to exist, they perform important functions, maintaining a measure of order and providing needed services. We show our respect for these authorities by means of our law-abiding conduct. We are careful to pay whatever taxes we owe, to fill out properly any forms or documents that the government may require, and to comply with any laws that involve us, our family, business, or possessions. However, we do not submit to the secular authorities if they ask us to disobey God. Rather, we reply as did the apostles of old: "We must obey God as ruler rather than men."—Acts 5:28, 29; see the box "Whose Authority Should I Obey?" on page 42.

[19] We also show respect for secular authorities by our demeanor. At times, we may deal directly with govern-

---

* On pages 209-12, the Appendix examines a few practical ways to apply this principle.

18, 19. (a) How would you explain the principles outlined at Romans 13:1-7? (b) How do we show respect for secular authorities?

ment officials. The apostle Paul dealt with such rulers as King Herod Agrippa and Governor Festus. These men were seriously flawed, but Paul addressed them with respect. (Acts 26:2, 25) We imitate Paul's example, whether the official we address is a powerful ruler or a local policeman. In school, young Christians endeavor to show similar respect for their teachers and for school officials and employees. Of course, we do not limit such respect to those who approve of our beliefs; we are also respectful when dealing with those who are antagonistic toward Jehovah's Witnesses. Really, nonbelievers in general should be able to sense our respect.—Romans 12:17, 18; 1 Peter 3:15.

[20] Let us not be stingy when it comes to showing respect. The apostle Peter wrote: "Honor men of all sorts." (1 Peter 2:17) When people sense that we view them with genuine respect, they may be deeply impressed. Remember, this quality is becoming ever rarer. Showing it, then, is one way in which we heed Jesus' command: "Let your light shine before men, that they may see your fine works and give glory to your Father who is in the heavens." —Matthew 5:16.

[21] In this bedarkened world, good-hearted people are drawn to spiritual light. So our showing respect in the family, in the congregation, and in secular settings may attract some and move them to walk in the light with us. What a glorious prospect! Even if that does not happen, though, one thing is sure. Our respect for humans pleases Jehovah God and helps us to remain in his love. What reward could be greater than that?

20, 21. What are some of the blessings that result from showing proper respect for authority?

"LISTEN TO COUNSEL AND ACCEPT DISCIPLINE"

Satan's spirit—his rebellious, contentious attitude—fills today's world. The Bible thus refers to Satan as "the ruler of the authority of the air" and mentions the resulting "spirit that now operates in the sons of disobedience." (Ephesians 2:2) Many today want to be completely independent of the authority of others. Sadly, that spirit of independence has even infected some in the Christian congregation. For example, an elder may offer some kindly counsel on the dangers of immoral or violent entertainment, but some may resist or even resent the counsel. Each of us needs to apply the words of Proverbs 19:20: "Listen to counsel and accept discipline, in order that you may become wise in your future."

What can help us in this regard? Consider three common reasons why people resist counsel or discipline, and then note the Scriptural viewpoint.

- "I don't think the counsel was appropriate." We may feel that the counsel does not really fit our circumstances or that the one giving it did not grasp the whole picture. Our immediate reaction might even be to belittle the counsel. (Hebrews 12:5) Since we are all imperfect, is it not possible that our own view of the matter is what needs adjusting? (Proverbs 19:3) Was there not *some* valid reason for the counsel to be given? Then that is what we need to focus on. God's Word advises us: "Take hold on discipline; do not let go. Safeguard it, for it itself is your life."—Proverbs 4:13.

- "I don't like the way the counsel was given." Granted, God's Word sets a high standard for the way counsel should be given. (Galatians 6:1) However, the Bible also says: "All have sinned and fall short of the glory of God." (Romans 3:23) The only way that we can ever receive perfect counsel delivered in just the right way is to receive it from a perfect person. (James 3:2) Jehovah uses imperfect humans to counsel us, so it is wise to avoid focusing on the way the counsel is given. Look, rather, to the content of the counsel, and prayerfully consider how to apply it.

- "He is in no position to counsel me!" If we think that personal faults in the counselor invalidate his counsel, we need to remember the points noted above. Likewise, if we think that our age, experience, or responsibilities in the congregation somehow put us above counsel, we need to readjust our thinking. In ancient Israel, the king had great responsibilities, yet he had to accept counsel from prophets, priests, and others who were among his subjects. (2 Samuel 12:1-13; 2 Chronicles 26:16-20) Today, Jehovah's organization appoints imperfect men to offer counsel, and mature Christians gladly accept it and apply it. If we have greater responsibilities or experience than others do, we should be even more conscious of the need to set an example in reasonableness and humility by accepting counsel and applying it.—1 Timothy 3:2, 3; Titus 3:2.

Clearly, none of us is above counsel. So let us be resolved to accept counsel readily, apply it obediently, and thank Jehovah heartily for this lifesaving gift. Counsel really is an expression of Jehovah's love for us, and we want to remain in God's love.—Hebrews 12:6-11.

"BE OBEDIENT TO THOSE WHO ARE TAKING THE LEAD"

In ancient Israel, there was an urgent need for organization. Moses alone could not oversee millions of people traveling together in a dangerous wilderness. What did he do? "Moses proceeded to choose capable men out of all Israel and to give them positions as heads over the people, as chiefs of thousands, chiefs of hundreds, chiefs of fifties and chiefs of tens."—Exodus 18:25.

In the Christian congregation today, there is a similar need for organization. That is why a book study group has an overseer, a congregation has elders, a group of congregations has a circuit overseer, a group of circuits has a district overseer, and a country has a Country Committee or a Branch Committee. Because of this organization, each man acting as a shepherd is able to pay close attention to Jehovah's sheep assigned to his care. Such shepherds are accountable to Jehovah and to Christ.—Acts 20:28.

This organizational arrangement calls for each of us to be obedient and submissive. Never would we want to have the attitude of Diotrephes, who had no respect for those taking the lead in his day. (3 John 9, 10) Rather, we want to heed the words of the apostle Paul, who wrote: "Be obedient to those who are taking the lead among you and be submissive, for they are keeping watch over your souls as those who will render an account; that they may do this with joy and not with sighing, for this would be damaging to you." (Hebrews 13:17) Some obey when they agree with the direction coming from those taking the lead but refuse to submit when they disagree with the direction or cannot see the reason for it. Keep in mind, though, that being submissive can include the idea that we obey even when we are not inclined to do so. Each of us, then, does well to ask himself, 'Am I obedient and submissive to those taking the lead over me?'

Of course, God's Word does not spell out every arrangement or procedure needed to help the congregation function. Yet, the Bible does say: "Let all things take place decently and by arrangement." (1 Corinthians 14:40) The Governing Body obeys this direction by putting in place various helpful procedures and guidelines that ensure the smooth and orderly operation of the congregation. Responsible Christian men do their part by setting an example of obedience as they put such arrangements into effect. They also show themselves "reasonable, ready to obey" those placed in oversight. (James 3:17) Thus, each book study, congregation, circuit, district, and country is blessed with a united, orderly body of believers who reflect well on the happy God.—1 Corinthians 14:33; 1 Timothy 1:11.

On the other hand, Paul's words found at Hebrews 13:17 also highlight why a disobedient spirit is harmful. It may cause those in positions of responsibility to do their work "with sighing." What should be considered a privilege of sacred service can feel like a burden when a brother must deal with an uncooperative, rebellious spirit in the flock. In turn, damage results "to you," the entire congregation. Of course, there is yet another form of damage that results when a person refuses to submit to theocratic order. It hurts his spirituality if he is too proud to submit, putting distance between him and his heavenly Father. (Psalm 138:6) Let us all, then, be determined to remain obedient and submissive.

CHAPTER 5

How to Keep Separate From the World

"You are no part of the world."
—JOHN 15:19.

DURING his final night on earth as a human, Jesus expressed deep concern for the future welfare of his followers. He even prayed about the matter, saying to his Father: "I request you, not to take them out of the world, but to watch over them because of the wicked one. They are no part of the world, just as I am no part of the world." (John 17:15, 16) In this heartfelt request, Jesus showed both his deep love for his followers and the importance of his words stated earlier that night to some of them: "You are no part of the world." (John 15:19) Clearly, it was of great importance to Jesus that his followers keep separate from the world!

² "The world" Jesus mentioned refers to all of mankind who are alienated from God, ruled by Satan, and enslaved to the selfish, prideful spirit that emanates from him. (John 14:30; Ephesians 2:2; 1 John 5:19) Indeed, "friendship with [that] world is enmity with God." (James 4:4) How, though, can all who want to remain in God's love be in the world yet be separate from it? We will consider five ways: by remaining loyal to God's Kingdom under Christ and neutral in worldly politics, by resisting the spirit of the world, by being modest in our

---

1. What did Jesus emphasize during his final night on earth as a human?
2. What is "the world" to which Jesus referred?

dress and grooming, by keeping our eye simple, and by putting on our spiritual suit of armor.

REMAINING LOYAL AND NEUTRAL

³ Instead of participating in the politics of his day, Jesus focused on preaching about God's Kingdom, the future heavenly government of which he was the prospective King. (Daniel 7:13, 14; Luke 4:43; 17:20, 21) Thus, when before Roman Governor Pontius Pilate, Jesus could say: "My kingdom is no part of this world." (John 18: 36) His faithful followers imitate his example by giving their loyalty to Christ and his Kingdom and by announcing that Kingdom to the world. (Matthew 24:14) "We are therefore ambassadors substituting for Christ," wrote the apostle Paul. "As substitutes for Christ we beg: 'Become reconciled to God.' "*—2 Corinthians 5:20.

⁴ Because ambassadors represent a foreign sovereign or state, they do not interfere in the internal affairs of the countries where they serve; they remain neutral. Ambassadors do, however, advocate the government of the country they represent. The same is true of Christ's anointed followers, whose "citizenship exists in the heavens." (Philippians 3:20) In fact, thanks to their zealous Kingdom preaching, they have helped millions of Christ's "other sheep" to "become reconciled to God."

---

* Since Pentecost 33 C.E., Christ has served as King over his congregation of anointed followers on earth. (Colossians 1:13) In 1914, Christ received royal authority over "the kingdom of the world." Hence, anointed Christians now also serve as ambassadors of the Messianic Kingdom.—Revelation 11:15.

---

3. (a) How did Jesus view the politics of his day? (b) Why can it be said that Jesus' anointed followers serve as ambassadors? (Include footnote.)
4. How have all true Christians demonstrated loyalty to God's Kingdom? (See the box on page 52.)

> ### EARLY CHRISTIAN NEUTRALS
>
> Secular history provides ample evidence that the early Christians remained politically neutral and refrained from warfare. Says the book *The Beginnings of Christianity:* "The founders of Christianity guarded with sedulous care against the development of anything like a disposition to interfere directly with the established political order." Similarly, the book *On the Road to Civilization* notes: "Early Christianity was little understood and was regarded with little favor by those who ruled the pagan world. . . . Christians refused to share certain duties of Roman citizens. . . . They would not hold political office."
>
> Regarding the early Christians and military service, German theologian Peter Meinhold said: "Being a Christian and a soldier was considered irreconcilable." In his essay "An Inquiry Into the Accordancy of War With the Principles of Christianity," religion writer Jonathan Dymond wrote that for some time after the death of Jesus, His followers "refused to engage in [war]; whatever were the consequences, whether reproach, or imprisonment, or death." Dymond added: "These facts are indisputable." Only when "Christianity became corrupted," said another writer, did Christians become soldiers.

(John 10:16; Matthew 25:31-40) These latter ones serve as Christ's envoys, as it were, in support of Jesus' anointed brothers. As one united flock advocating the Messianic Kingdom, both groups maintain strict neutrality toward the world's political affairs.—Isaiah 2:2-4.

How to Keep Separate From the World

⁵ Loyalty to Christ is not the only reason that true Christians are neutral. Unlike ancient Israel, which had a God-given land allocation, we are part of an international brotherhood. (Matthew 28:19; 1 Peter 2:9) Thus, if we were to rally to the side of local political parties, both our freeness of speech in regard to the Kingdom message and our Christian unity would be severely compromised. (1 Corinthians 1:10) Furthermore, during war time, we would be fighting against fellow believers, whom we are commanded to love. (John 13:34, 35; 1 John 3:10-12) With good reason, then, Jesus told his disciples to lay down the sword. And he even told them to love their enemies.—Matthew 5:44; 26:52; see the box "Am I Remaining Neutral?" on page 55.

⁶ As true Christians, we have dedicated our life to God, not to any human, human institution, or nation. Says 1 Corinthians 6:19, 20: "You do not belong to yourselves, for you were bought with a price." Thus, while rendering "Caesar" his due in the form of honor, taxes, and relative subjection, Jesus' followers give "God's things to God." (Mark 12:17; Romans 13:1-7) This includes their worship, their whole-souled love, and their loyal obedience. If necessary, they are ready to give up their life for God.—Luke 4:8; 10:27; Acts 5:29; Romans 14:8.

RESISTING "THE SPIRIT OF THE WORLD"

⁷ Another way that Christians keep separate from the world is by resisting its evil spirit. "We received, not the

---

5. How is the Christian congregation different from ancient Israel, and how does this difference manifest itself?
6. How does your dedication to God affect your relationship with Caesar?
7, 8. What is "the spirit of the world," and how does that spirit "operate" in a person?

spirit of the world, but the spirit which is from God," wrote Paul. (1 Corinthians 2:12) To the Ephesians, he said: "You at one time walked according to . . . this world, according to the ruler of the authority of the air, the spirit that now operates in the sons of disobedience."—Ephesians 2:2, 3.

⁸ The world's "air," or spirit, is an invisible, impelling force that incites disobedience to God and fosters "the desire of the flesh and the desire of the eyes." (1 John 2:16; 1 Timothy 6:9, 10) The "authority" of this spirit lies in its appeal to the sinful flesh, its subtlety, its relentlessness and, like air, its pervasiveness. Moreover, it "operates" in a person by gradually nurturing in him ungodly traits, such as selfishness, haughtiness, greedy ambition, and the spirit of moral independence and rebellion.* Simply put, the spirit of the world progressively causes the traits of the Devil to grow in the heart of a man. —John 8:44; Acts 13:10; 1 John 3:8, 10.

⁹ Can the spirit of the world take root in your mind and heart? Yes, but only if you let it do so by lowering your guard. (Proverbs 4:23) Its influence often begins subtly, perhaps by way of associates who may appear to be good people but, in fact, have no love for Jehovah. (Proverbs 13:20; 1 Corinthians 15:33) You can also absorb that evil spirit through objectionable literature, pornographic or apostate Internet sites, unwholesome entertainment, and highly competitive sports—really, through anyone or anything that conveys the thinking of Satan or his system.

---

* See *Reasoning From the Scriptures*, pages 389-93, published by Jehovah's Witnesses.

---

9. In what ways can the world's spirit enter our mind and heart?

¹⁰ How can we resist the insidious spirit of the world and keep ourselves in God's love? Only by taking full advantage of Jehovah's spiritual provisions and by praying constantly for holy spirit. Jehovah is far greater than the Devil or the wicked world under satanic control. (1 John 4:4) How important, then, that we stay close to Jehovah in prayer!

---

10. How can we resist the spirit of the world?

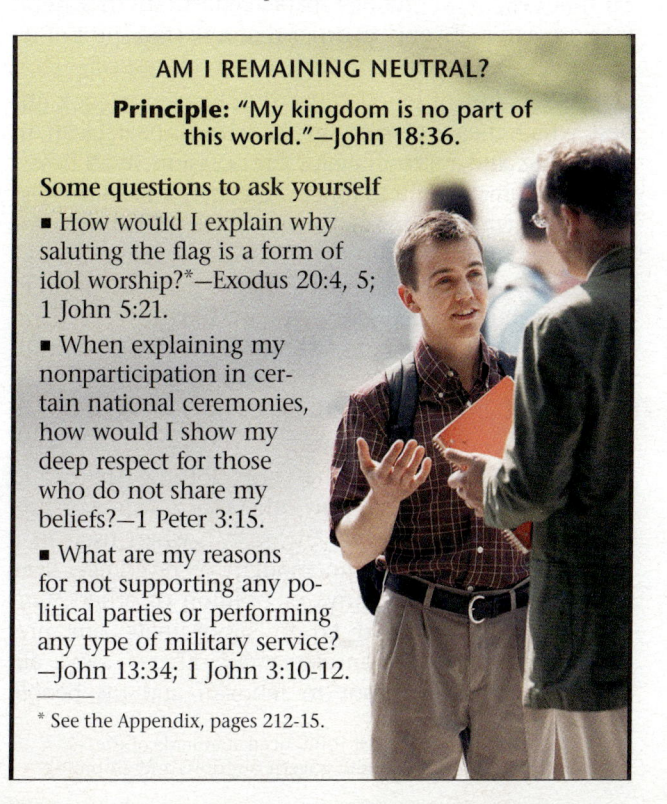

AM I REMAINING NEUTRAL?

Principle: "My kingdom is no part of this world."—John 18:36.

Some questions to ask yourself

- How would I explain why saluting the flag is a form of idol worship?*—Exodus 20:4, 5; 1 John 5:21.

- When explaining my nonparticipation in certain national ceremonies, how would I show my deep respect for those who do not share my beliefs?—1 Peter 3:15.

- What are my reasons for not supporting any political parties or performing any type of military service? —John 13:34; 1 John 3:10-12.

---

* See the Appendix, pages 212-15.

BEING MODEST IN OUR DRESS AND GROOMING

¹¹ An outward indication of the spirit that impels a person is his dress, grooming, and hygiene. In many lands, standards of dress have fallen so low that one television commentator suggested that soon there will be nothing left for prostitutes to wear. Even girls not yet in their teens have been caught up in this trend—"long on skin, short on modesty," said one newspaper report. Another trend is to dress in a slovenly manner that reflects a spirit of rebellion as well as a lack of dignity and self-respect.

¹² As servants of Jehovah, we rightly want to look our best, which means dressing in a way that is neat, clean, in good taste, and appropriate for the occasion. At all times, our appearance ought to reflect "modesty and soundness of mind," which along with "good works" is fitting for anyone—male or female—"professing to reverence God." Of course, our main concern is, not to draw attention to ourselves, but to "keep [ourselves] in God's love." (1 Timothy 2:9, 10; Jude 21) Yes, we want our most beautiful adornment to be "the secret person of the heart . . . , which is of great value in the eyes of God."—1 Peter 3: 3, 4.

¹³ Keep in mind, too, that our clothing styles and grooming can influence how others view true worship. The Greek word rendered "modesty," when used in a moral sense, expresses the thought of reverence, awe, and respect for the feelings or opinion of others. Our goal, therefore, should be to subordinate our presumed rights to the consciences of others. Above all, we want to bring honor to Jehovah and his people

---

11. How has the world's spirit influenced standards of dress?
12, 13. What principles should govern our dress and grooming?

and to recommend ourselves as God's ministers, doing "all things for God's glory."—1 Corinthians 4:9; 10:31; 2 Corinthians 6:3, 4; 7:1.

¹⁴ Our dress, grooming, and cleanliness are even more important when we are engaging in the field ministry or attending a Christian meeting. Ask yourself: 'Do my appearance and personal hygiene draw undue attention to me? Do they embarrass others? Do I consider my rights in these areas to be more important than qualifying for service privileges in the congregation?' —Psalm 68:6; Philippians 4:5; 1 Peter 5:6.

Does my appearance bring honor to Jehovah?

¹⁵ The Bible does not set out for Christians a list of rules on dress, grooming, and hygiene. Jehovah has no desire to deny us our freedom of choice or the use of our thinking faculties. Rather, he wants us to become mature people who reason on Bible principles and who "through use have their perceptive powers trained to distinguish both right and wrong." (Hebrews 5:14) Above all, he wants us to be governed by love—love for God and neighbor. (Mark 12:30, 31) Within those boundaries, there is

---

14. In regard to our appearance and hygiene, what questions should we ask ourselves?
15. Why does God's Word not set out a list of rules on dress, grooming, and hygiene?

the potential for great variety in dress and grooming. Evidence of this can be seen in the colorfully dressed, joyful throngs of Jehovah's people no matter where on earth they are gathered.

KEEPING OUR EYE "SIMPLE"

¹⁶ The spirit of the world is deceptive and impels millions to look to money and material things for happiness. However, Jesus said: "Even when a person has an abundance his life does not result from the things he possesses." (Luke 12:15) While not endorsing asceticism, or extreme self-denial, Jesus taught that life and genuine happiness come to those who are "conscious of their spiritual need" and those who maintain a "simple" eye,

---

16. How does the spirit of the world run contrary to Jesus' teaching, and what questions should we ask ourselves?

one that is sincere and in sharp focus spiritually. (Matthew 5:3; 6:22, 23) Ask yourself: 'Do I truly believe what Jesus taught, or am I being influenced by "the father of the lie"? (John 8:44) What do my words, my goals, my priorities, and my way of life reveal?'—Luke 6:45; 21:34-36; 2 John 6.

¹⁷ "Wisdom is proved righteous by its works," said Jesus. (Matthew 11:19) Consider just some of the benefits enjoyed by those who maintain a simple eye. They find true refreshment in Kingdom service. (Matthew 11:29, 30) They avoid undue anxieties and thus spare themselves much mental and emotional pain. (1 Timothy 6:9, 10) Content with having life's necessities, they have more time for their family and Christian companions. They may sleep better as a result. (Ecclesiastes 5:12) They experience the greater joy of giving, doing so in whatever way they can. (Acts 20:35) And they "abound in hope" and have inner peace and contentment. (Romans 15:13; Matthew 6:31, 32) These blessings are truly priceless!

TAKING UP "THE COMPLETE SUIT OF ARMOR"

¹⁸ Those who keep themselves in God's love also enjoy spiritual protection from Satan, who wants to deprive Christians, not just of happiness, but of everlasting life. (1 Peter 5:8) "We have a wrestling," said Paul, "not against blood and flesh, but against the governments, against the authorities, against the world rulers of this darkness, against the wicked spirit forces in the heavenly places." (Ephesians 6:12) The word "wrestling" suggests that our fight is not long-distance—from

---

17. Name some benefits enjoyed by those who maintain a simple eye.
18. How does the Bible describe our enemy, his methods, and the nature of our struggle?

the safety of a hidden bunker, so to speak—but hand-to-hand. Furthermore, the terms "governments," "authorities," and "world rulers" indicate that attacks from the spirit realm are highly organized and deliberate.

[19] Despite human frailties and limitations, however, we can gain the victory. How? By taking up "the complete suit of armor from God." (Ephesians 6:13) Describing that armor, Ephesians 6:14-18 reads: "Stand firm, therefore, with your loins girded about with truth, and having on the breastplate of righteousness, and with your feet shod with the equipment of the good news of peace. Above all things, take up the large shield of faith, with which you will be able to quench all the wicked one's burning missiles. Also, accept the helmet [or, hope] of salvation, and the sword of the spirit, that is, God's word, while with every form of prayer and supplication you carry on prayer on every occasion in spirit."

[20] Since it is a provision of God, that spiritual suit of armor will not fail us, provided that we wear it at all times. Unlike literal soldiers, who may have long breaks from fighting, Christians are in a relentless life-and-death struggle that will not stop until God has destroyed Satan's world and abyssed all wicked spirits. (Revelation 12:17; 20:1-3) So do not give up if you are struggling with weaknesses or wrong desires, for we all have to "pummel" ourselves in order to stay faithful to Jehovah. (1 Corinthians 9:27) Indeed, it is when we are *not* wrestling that we should be concerned!

[21] Moreover, we cannot win this fight in our own strength. Hence, Paul reminds us of the need to pray to

---

19. Describe the Christian's spiritual suit of armor.
20. How does our situation differ from that of a literal soldier?
21. How only can we come off victorious in our spiritual warfare?

Jehovah "on every occasion in spirit." At the same time, we should listen to Jehovah by studying his Word and associating with fellow "soldiers" at every opportunity, for we are not in this fight alone! (Philemon 2; Hebrews 10: 24, 25) Those who are faithful in all these areas will not only come off victorious but will also be able to make a strong defense for their faith when it is challenged.

BE READY TO DEFEND YOUR FAITH

22 "Because you are no part of the world," said Jesus, "the world hates you." (John 15:19) Christians, therefore, must always be ready to defend their faith and to do so in a respectful, mild manner. (1 Peter 3:15) Ask yourself: 'Do I understand why Jehovah's Witnesses sometimes take a stand that is contrary to popular opinion? When facing the challenge of taking such a stand, am I thoroughly convinced that what the Bible and the faithful slave class say is right? (Matthew 24:45; John 17: 17) And when it comes to doing what is right in Jehovah's eyes, am I not only prepared to be different but also proud to be different?'—Psalm 34:2; Matthew 10: 32, 33.

23 Often, though, our desire to keep separate from the world is put to the test in more subtle ways. For example, as mentioned earlier, the Devil tries to lure Jehovah's servants into the world by means of worldly entertainment. How can we choose wholesome entertainment that will leave us refreshed and with a clean conscience? That subject will be considered in the next chapter.

22, 23. (a) Why must we be ready at all times to defend our faith, and what questions should we ask ourselves? (b) What subject will be considered in the next chapter?

CHAPTER 6

How to Choose Wholesome Entertainment

"Do all things for God's glory."
—1 CORINTHIANS 10:31.

IMAGINE that you are about to eat a tasty piece of fruit but then notice that a part of it is rotten. What will you do? Well, you could eat the entire fruit, even the bad part; you could throw away the entire fruit, including the bad part; or you could cut the bad part out of the fruit and enjoy the good part. What choice will you make?

² In a way, entertainment is like that fruit. At times, you want to enjoy some recreation, but you realize that much of the entertainment available today is morally bad, even rotten. So, what will you do? Some might tolerate what is bad and swallow whatever entertainment this world has to offer. Others might avoid all entertainment to make sure that they will not be exposed to anything harmful. Still others might carefully avoid entertainment that is harmful but occasionally enjoy that which is relatively wholesome. What choice should you make in order to keep yourself in God's love?

³ Most of us would select the third option. We appreciate the need for some recreation but want to limit our entertainment to what is morally sound. Therefore, we need to consider how we can determine what is wholesome and what is not. First, though, let us discuss what

---

1, 2. What choice do we need to make regarding entertainment?
3. What will we now consider?

"DO ALL THINGS FOR GOD'S GLORY"

⁴ Some time ago, an elderly Witness who was baptized in 1946 observed: "I have made it a point to be present at every baptism talk and to listen carefully, as if it were my own baptism." Why? He explained, "Keeping my dedication fresh has been an important step in remaining faithful." You will doubtless agree with that sentiment. Reminding yourself that you promised Jehovah you would use your entire life to serve him motivates you to endure. (Ecclesiastes 5:4; Hebrews 10:7) In fact, meditating on your dedication will affect your view not only of the Christian ministry but also of all other areas of life—including entertainment. The apostle Paul underlined that truth when he wrote to Christians in his day: "Whether you are eating or drinking or doing anything else, do *all things* for God's glory."—1 Corinthians 10:31.

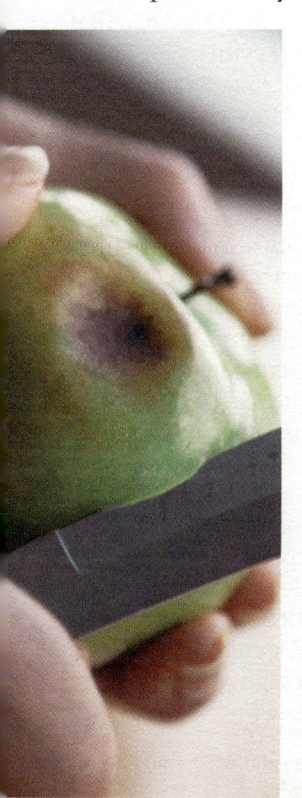

⁵ Everything you do in life is related to your worship of Jehovah.

---
4. How should our dedication affect our choice of entertainment?
5. How does Leviticus 22:18-20 help us to see the implicit warning behind Romans 12:1?

In his letter to the Romans, Paul used a forceful expression to impress this truth upon fellow believers. He urged them: "Present your bodies a sacrifice living, holy, acceptable to God, a sacred service with your power of reason." (Romans 12:1) Your body includes your mind, your heart, and your physical strength. All of these, you use in serving God. (Mark 12:30) Paul speaks of such whole-souled service as a sacrifice. That expression contains an implicit warning. Under the Mosaic Law, a sacrifice that was blemished was rejected by God. (Leviticus 22:18-20) Similarly, if a Christian's spiritual sacrifice is tainted in some way, it will be rejected by God. How, though, could that happen?

6 Paul admonished the Christians in Rome: "Do not . . . go on presenting your members ['parts of your body,' *New International Version*] to sin." Paul also told them to "put the practices of the body to death." (Romans 6:12-14; 8:13) Earlier in his letter, he had given some examples of such "practices of the body." Regarding sinful mankind, we read: "Their *mouth* is full of cursing." "Their *feet* are speedy to shed blood." "There is no fear of God before their *eyes*." (Romans 3:13-18) A Christian would blemish his body if he used his "members," or body parts, for such sinful practices. For instance, if a Christian today deliberately views such depraved material as pornography or watches sadistic violence, he is "presenting [his eyes] to sin" and is thus tainting his whole body. Any worship that he renders amounts to a sacrifice that is no longer holy and is unacceptable to God. (Deuteronomy 15:21; 1 Peter 1:14-16; 2 Peter 3:11) What a high price to pay for pursuing unwholesome entertainment!

6, 7. How could a Christian taint his body, and what could be the consequences?

⁷ Clearly, a Christian's choice of entertainment has weighty consequences. Surely, then, we want to choose entertainment that will enhance, not taint, our sacrifice to God. Let us now discuss how we can determine what is wholesome and what is not.

"ABHOR WHAT IS WICKED"

⁸ In broad terms, entertainment can be divided into two categories. One includes entertainment that Christians definitely avoid; the other is made up of entertainment that Christians may or may not find acceptable. Let us start by considering the first category—entertainment that Christians avoid.

⁹ As noted in Chapter 1, some forms of entertainment highlight activities expressly condemned in the Bible. Think, for example, of Web sites as well as movies, TV programs, and music that have sadistic or demonistic content or that contain pornography or promote vile, immoral practices. Since such degraded forms of entertainment portray in a positive light activities that violate Bible principles or break Bible laws, they should be shunned by true Christians. (Acts 15:28, 29; 1 Corinthians 6:9, 10; Revelation 21:8) By rejecting such unwholesome entertainment, you prove to Jehovah that you truly "abhor what is wicked" and consistently "turn away from what is bad." That way, you have "faith without hypocrisy."—Romans 12:9; Psalm 34:14; 1 Timothy 1:5.

¹⁰ Some may feel, though, that indulging in entertainment that graphically portrays immoral behavior is

---

8, 9. (a) Entertainment can be broadly divided into what two categories? (b) What forms of entertainment do we reject, and why?
10. What sort of reasoning about entertainment is dangerous, and why?

harmless. They reason, 'I may watch it in movies or on TV, but I would never do such things myself.' Such reasoning is deceptive and dangerous. (Jeremiah 17:9) If we find it entertaining to watch what Jehovah condemns, do we really "abhor what is wicked"? Repeatedly exposing ourselves to wicked conduct will dull our senses. (Psalm 119:70; 1 Timothy 4:1, 2) Such a practice could affect what we do or how we view the sinful conduct of others.

¹¹ This has actually happened. Some Christians have committed immoral acts because they were influenced by the entertainment that they habitually watched. They learned the hard way that "whatever a man is sowing, this he will also reap." (Galatians 6:7) But such a sad outcome can be avoided. If you carefully sow in your mind what is sound, you will happily reap in your life what is wholesome.—See the box "What Entertainment Should I Choose?" on page 67.

PERSONAL DECISIONS BASED ON BIBLE PRINCIPLES

¹² Let us now discuss the second category—entertainment that features activities that are neither directly condemned nor expressly approved in God's Word. When choosing from such entertainment, each Christian needs to make a personal decision as to what he finds wholesome. (Galatians 6:5) However, when faced with this choice, we are not without guidance. The Bible contains principles, or fundamental truths, that enable us to perceive Jehovah's way of thinking. By paying attention to

---

11. How has Galatians 6:7 proved true in regard to entertainment?
12. How does Galatians 6:5 relate to entertainment, and what guidance do we have for making personal decisions?

WHAT ENTERTAINMENT SHOULD I CHOOSE?

Principle: "Abhor what is wicked, cling to what is good."—Romans 12:9.

Would God be pleased if . . .

- the lyrics of the music I listen to make it difficult for me to keep my mind on chaste things? —1 Corinthians 6:9, 10.

- I imitate the negative speech and actions of people in the movies I choose to watch?—Luke 6:40.

- I choose to play video games that require me to act the part of a violent or an immoral person? —Psalm 11:5, 7.

- the standards that I preach to others are not the standards that I use to guide me in my choice of entertainment?—Romans 2:21.

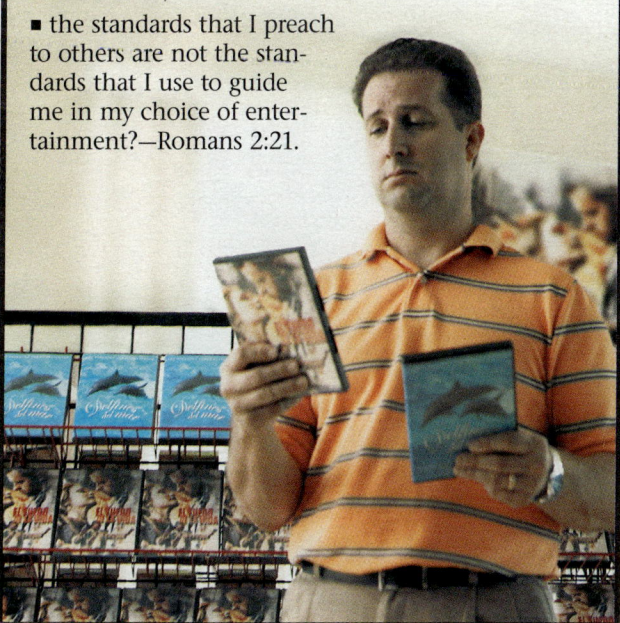

such principles, we will be able to perceive "what the will of Jehovah is" in all things, including our choice of entertainment.—Ephesians 5:17.

[13] Understandably, not all Christians have developed their moral perception, or discernment, to the same degree. (Philippians 1:9) Moreover, Christians realize that in the area of entertainment, tastes vary. Therefore, it is

---

13. What will move us to avoid entertainment that could displease Jehovah?

Applying godly principles when choosing entertainment protects us from spiritual harm

not to be expected that all Christians will make exactly the same decisions. Even so, the more we allow godly principles to influence our mind and heart, the more eager we will be to avoid any form of entertainment that could displease Jehovah.—Psalm 119:11, 129; 1 Peter 2:16.

[14] When choosing entertainment, there is another important factor to consider: your time. While the content of your entertainment reveals what you find acceptable, the amount of time you spend on it reveals what you find important. For Christians, of course, spiritual matters are the most important. (Matthew 6:33) What, then, can you do to make sure that Kingdom interests remain first in your life? The apostle Paul stated: "Keep strict watch that how you walk is not as unwise but as wise persons, buying out the opportune time for yourselves." (Ephesians 5:15, 16) Indeed, setting clear limits on the amount of time you set aside for entertainment will help you to have the needed time available for "the more important things"—activities that contribute to your spiritual well-being.—Philippians 1:10.

[15] It is also wise to allow a margin of safety when choosing entertainment. What does that mean? Consider once more the example of the fruit. To avoid inadvertently eating what is rotten, you cut out not just the exact area that is bad but also a margin around it. Similarly, it is wise to apply a safety margin in choosing entertainment. A wise Christian avoids not only entertainment that is clearly in violation of Bible principles but also

---

14. (a) What factor should we consider when choosing entertainment? (b) How can we keep Kingdom interests first in life?
15. Why is it wise to allow a margin of safety when choosing entertainment?

"WHATEVER THINGS ARE CHASTE"

16 When choosing entertainment, true Christians first of all take into account Jehovah's view. The Bible reveals Jehovah's feelings and standards. For instance, King Solomon lists several things that Jehovah hates, such as "a false tongue, and hands that are shedding innocent blood, a heart fabricating hurtful schemes, feet that are in a hurry to run to badness." (Proverbs 6:16-19) How should Jehovah's view affect yours? "O you lovers of Jehovah," exhorts the psalmist, "hate what is bad." (Psalm 97:10) Your choices in entertainment need to show that you truly do hate what Jehovah hates. (Galatians 5:19-21) Keep in mind, too, that what you do in private, more so than in public, reveals what kind of person you really are. (Psalm 11:4; 16:8) Hence, if you have a heartfelt desire to reflect in all aspects of your life Jehovah's feelings on moral matters, you will always make choices in accord with Bible principles. Doing so will become your way of life.—2 Corinthians 3:18.

16. (a) How may we show that we have Jehovah's view on morals? (b) How can applying Bible principles become your way of life?

Before choosing a form of entertainment, Christians ask themselves

- How will it affect my relationship with God?
- How will it affect me personally?
- How will it affect others?

¹⁷ What more can you do to ensure that you will act in harmony with Jehovah's way of thinking when choosing entertainment? Reflect on the question, 'How will this affect me and my standing with God?' For instance, before deciding whether to watch a certain movie, ask yourself, 'How will the content of this movie affect my conscience?' Let us consider what principles have a bearing on that subject.

¹⁸ A key principle is found at Philippians 4:8, which states: "Whatever things are true, whatever things are of serious concern, whatever things are righteous, whatever things are chaste, whatever things are lovable, whatever things are well spoken of, whatever virtue there is and whatever praiseworthy thing there is, *continue considering these things.*" Granted, Paul was discussing, not entertainment, but the meditations of the heart, which should center on things that please God. (Psalm 19:14) Yet, Paul's words can be applied in principle to the matter of entertainment. How?

¹⁹ Ask yourself, 'Does my choice of movies, video games, music, or other forms of entertainment fill my mind with "whatever things are chaste"?' For instance, after you watch a movie, what mental images are left dominating your mind? If they are pleasant, pure, and refreshing, then you know that your entertainment was wholesome. However, if the movie you watched makes you think about things that are unchaste, then your entertainment was unsound, even harmful.

---

17. Before choosing entertainment, what questions should we ask?
18, 19. (a) How can the principle found at Philippians 4:8 help us to determine whether our entertainment is wholesome? (b) What other principles can help you to select good entertainment? (See footnote.)

(Matthew 12:33; Mark 7:20-23) Why? Because thinking about things that are morally unclean disturbs your inner peace, scars your Bible-trained conscience, and can ruin your relationship with God. (Ephesians 5:5; 1 Timothy 1:5, 19) Since such entertainment has a harmful effect on you personally, be determined to avoid it.* (Romans 12:2) Be like the psalmist who prayed to Jehovah: "Make my eyes pass on from seeing what is worthless." —Psalm 119:37.

SEEK THE ADVANTAGE OF OTHERS

20 Paul mentioned a key Bible principle that needs to be taken into account when making decisions on personal matters. He stated: "All things are lawful; but not all things build up. Let each one keep seeking, not his own advantage, but that of the other person." (1 Corinthians 10:23, 24) How does that principle relate to choosing wholesome entertainment? You need to ask yourself, 'How will the entertainment that I choose affect others?'

21 Your conscience may allow you to enjoy a certain form of entertainment that you view as "lawful," or acceptable. However, if you notice that other believers with a more restrictive conscience find it objectionable, you may decide not to pursue it. Why? Because you do not want to "sin against your brothers"—or even be "sinning against Christ," as Paul stated—by making it more difficult for your fellow believers to maintain faithfulness to God. You take to heart the admonition: "Keep from becoming causes for stumbling." (1 Corinthians 8:12;

---

* Some more principles applicable to entertainment are found at Proverbs 3:31; 13:20; Ephesians 5:3, 4; and Colossians 3:5, 8, 20.

20, 21. How does 1 Corinthians 10:23, 24 relate to choosing wholesome entertainment?

10:32) True Christians today heed Paul's considerate and perceptive counsel by avoiding entertainment that may be "lawful" but does not "build up."—Romans 14:1; 15:1.

²² There is, though, another side to the matter of seeking the advantage of others. A Christian with a more restrictive conscience should not insist that all in the Christian congregation conform to his narrower view on what is proper entertainment. If he were to do so, he would be like a driver on a highway who insists that all other drivers using the same road hold to the same speed that he prefers. Such a demand would not be reasonable. Out of Christian love, someone with a more confining conscience needs to respect fellow believers whose views on entertainment differ somewhat from his own but are still within the bounds of Christian principles. That way, he lets his "reasonableness become known to all men."—Philippians 4:5; Ecclesiastes 7:16.

²³ In short, how can you make sure that you choose wholesome entertainment? Reject any kind of entertainment that graphically portrays degraded, immoral activities that are expressly condemned in God's Word. Follow Bible principles that can be applied to types of entertainment that are not specifically mentioned in the Bible. Avoid entertainment that injures your conscience, and be willing to forgo forms of entertainment that might wound the sensitivities of others, especially those of fellow believers. May your firm decision to do so bring glory to God and keep you and your family in his love.

---

22. Why do Christians allow room for different views in personal matters?
23. How can you make sure that you choose wholesome entertainment?

CHAPTER 7

Do You Value Life as God Does?

"With you is the source of life."
—PSALM 36:9.

OUR heavenly Father has given us a priceless possession —the gift of life as intelligent humans who are capable of reflecting his qualities. (Genesis 1:27) Thanks to that precious gift, we are able to reason on Bible principles. By applying them, we can grow into spiritually mature people who love Jehovah and whose "perceptive powers [have been] trained to distinguish both right and wrong."—Hebrews 5:14.

² The ability to reason on Bible principles is especially important today, for the world has become so complex that no amount of laws could cover every possible situation that might arise in life. Medical science well illustrates this point, especially in regard to products and procedures involving blood. This is an area of interest and concern to all who want to obey Jehovah. Still, if we understand the relevant Bible principles, we should be able to make wise decisions that both satisfy our conscience and keep us in God's love. (Proverbs 2:6-11) Consider some of these principles.

LIFE AND BLOOD ARE SACRED

³ Jehovah first disclosed the intimate connection be-

1, 2. What gift from God is especially valuable today, and why so?
3, 4. When was the sanctity of blood introduced in the Scriptures, and upon what principles does it rest?

tween life and blood, as well as their sanctity, or sacredness, shortly after Cain murdered Abel. "Listen!" God said to Cain. "Your brother's blood is crying out to me from the ground." (Genesis 4:10) In Jehovah's eyes, Abel's blood represented his life, which had been brutally cut short. So, in a sense, Abel's blood cried out to God for vengeance.—Hebrews 12:24.

[4] After the Noachian Flood, God gave humans permission to eat the flesh of animals but not the blood. God stated: "Only flesh with its soul—its blood—you must not eat. And, besides that, your blood of your souls shall I ask back." (Genesis 9:4, 5) This command applies to all of Noah's descendants right down to our day. It reaffirms what was implied in God's earlier words to Cain—that the soul, or life, of all creatures is represented by the blood. That decree also establishes that Jehovah, the Source of life, will hold to account all humans who disrespect life and blood.—Psalm 36:9.

[5] These two fundamental truths were reflected in the Mosaic Law. Leviticus 17:10, 11 reads: "As for any man ... who eats any sort of blood, I shall certainly set my face against the soul that is eating the blood, and I shall indeed cut him off from among his people. For the soul of the flesh is in the blood, and I myself have put it upon the altar for you to make atonement for your souls, because it is the blood that makes atonement by the soul in it."*
—See the box "The Atoning Power of Blood," on page 76.

---

* Concerning God's statement, "the soul of the flesh is in the blood," the journal *Scientific American* notes: "Metaphorical significance aside, the statement is literally true: each type of blood cell is required for life."

5, 6. How did the Mosaic Law show that blood is both sacred and precious? (See also the box on page 78.)

> ## THE ATONING POWER OF BLOOD
>
> In God's Word, blood is considered to be equivalent to life. Hence, instead of being condemned because he broke Jehovah's commandments, a repentant sinner in ancient Israel could offer an animal sacrifice on God's altar. (Leviticus 4:27-31) This sacrifice atoned for his sins but only in a provisional way.
>
> As used in the Bible, "atonement" conveys the thought of "exchange" or "cover," as the right lid, for example, would properly cover a container. Of course, no animal could perfectly "cover," or atone for, the sins of a human. Animal sacrifices did, however, provide a shadow of the perfect atonement sacrifice to come.—Hebrews 10:1, 4.
>
> That atonement was provided "through the offering of the body of Jesus Christ once for all time." (Hebrews 10:10) Christ's perfect human life, represented by his "precious blood, like that of an unblemished and spotless lamb," corresponded exactly to the life that Adam lost. (1 Peter 1:19) Thus, in an exquisitely beautiful and loving way, justice was satisfied and our "everlasting deliverance" was made possible.—Hebrews 9:11, 12; John 3:16; Revelation 7:14.

⁶ If the blood of a slaughtered animal was not used on the altar, it was to be poured out on the ground. Thus, in a symbolic way, the life was returned to its original Owner. (Deuteronomy 12:16; Ezekiel 18:4) Note, though, that the Israelites did not have to go to extremes in trying to remove every trace of blood from the animal's tissues. Provided that the creature was properly slaughtered and bled,

Do You Value Life as God Does? 77

an Israelite could eat it with a clear conscience, as due respect would have been accorded to the Life-Giver.

⁷ David, "a man agreeable to [God's] heart," grasped the principles behind God's law on blood. (Acts 13:22) On one occasion when he was very thirsty, three of his men forced their way into the enemy camp, drew water from a cistern, and brought it to him. How did David react? "Shall I drink the blood of the men going at the risk of their souls?" he asked. In David's eyes, the water was, in effect, the lifeblood of his men. So despite his thirst, he "poured it out to Jehovah."—2 Samuel 23:15-17.

⁸ Some 2,400 years after the Noachian decree and about 1,500 years after the Law covenant was made, Jehovah inspired the governing body of the early Christian congregation to write: "The holy spirit and we ourselves have favored adding no further burden to you, except these necessary things, to keep abstaining from things sacrificed to idols and from blood and from things strangled and from fornication."—Acts 15:28, 29.

⁹ Clearly, the early governing body discerned that blood is sacred and that misusing it is as morally wrong as committing idolatry or fornication. True Christians today accept that stand. Moreover, because they think in terms of Bible principles, they are able to please Jehovah when making decisions about the use of blood.

THE MEDICAL USE OF BLOOD

¹⁰ Jehovah's Witnesses recognize that "abstaining from . . . blood" means not accepting blood transfusions and

---

7. How did David show respect for the sanctity of blood?
8, 9. Did God's view of life and blood change with the establishment of the Christian congregation? Explain.
10, 11. (a) How do Jehovah's Witnesses view the transfusion of whole blood and primary blood components? (b) In what areas regarding blood might Christians have differing opinions?

> ### RESPECT THE LIFE OF ANIMALS
>
> Although Jehovah allows us to kill animals for food and clothing or to protect ourselves from harm, we must exercise that authority in a balanced, kind way. (Genesis 3:21; 9:3) We do not want to be like the cruel hunter Nimrod, who apparently killed animals for the sheer thrill of it. (Genesis 10:9) Rather, we should imitate Jehovah, who is interested in the welfare of all animals, even tiny sparrows.—Jonah 4:11; Matthew 10:29.
>
> God's interest was reflected in the Mosaic Law. (Exodus 23:4, 5, 12; Deuteronomy 22:10; 25:4) In harmony with that Law, Proverbs 12:10 states: "The righteous one is caring for the soul of his domestic animal, but the mercies of the wicked ones are cruel." Soon both the cruel and their ways will be things of the past.

not donating or storing their own blood for transfusion. Out of respect for God's law, they also do not accept the four primary components of blood: red cells, white cells, platelets, and plasma.

[11] Today, through further processing, these components are often broken down into fractions that are used in a variety of ways. Could a Christian accept such fractions? Does he view them as "blood"? Each one must personally decide on this matter. The same applies to such medical procedures as hemodialysis, hemodilution, and cell salvage involving one's own blood, provided that it has not been stored.—See the Appendix, pages 215-18.

[12] Are matters for personal decision of little importance

---

12. How should we view and handle matters of conscience?

to Jehovah? No, for he is keenly interested in our thoughts and motivations. (Proverbs 17:3; 21:2; 24:12) So after doing prayerful research on a medical product or procedure, we should heed our Bible-trained conscience. (Romans 14:2, 22, 23) Of course, others should not impose their conscience on us, nor should we ask, "What would you do if you were in my situation?" In such matters, each Christian should "carry his own load."*—Galatians 6:5; Romans 14:12; see the box "Do I View Blood as Sacred?" on page 81.

JEHOVAH'S LAWS REFLECT HIS FATHERLY LOVE

13 The laws and principles found in the Bible reveal Jehovah to be both a wise Legislator and a loving Father who deeply cares about the welfare of his children. (Psalm 19:7-11) Although the command to "abstain from . . . blood" was not given as a health regulation, it does shield us from complications related to blood transfusions. (Acts 15:20) In fact, many in the medical field rate bloodless surgery as the "gold standard" of modern medical care. To true Christians, such developments simply confirm Jehovah's unfathomable wisdom and fatherly love.—Isaiah 55:9; John 14:21, 23.

14 God's concern for the welfare of his people in ancient Israel was reflected in many of his laws. For example, he required that Israelite houses have a parapet around the roof to prevent accidents, since roofs were places of considerable activity. (Deuteronomy 22:8; 1 Samuel 9:

---

* See *Awake!* of August 2006, pages 3-12, published by Jehovah's Witnesses.

13. What do Jehovah's laws and principles reveal about him? Illustrate.
14, 15. (a) God's love for his people was reflected in what laws? (b) How can you apply the principles behind these safety regulations?

25, 26; Nehemiah 8:16; Acts 10:9) God also commanded that dangerous bulls be kept under guard. (Exodus 21:28, 29) To ignore these requirements showed a gross lack of respect for the welfare of others and could have resulted in bloodguilt.

[15] How can you apply the principles underlying these laws? Why not think about your vehicle, your driving habits, your animals, your home, your place of work, and your choice of recreation? In some lands, accidents are the leading cause of death among the young, often because they take needless risks. However, young ones who want to remain in God's love value life and do not seek excitement in dangerous activities. They do not foolishly think that youth spells invulnerability. Rather, they enjoy their youth by warding off needless calamity.—Ecclesiastes 11:9, 10.

[16] Even the life of the unborn is precious in God's eyes. In ancient Israel, if someone harmed a pregnant woman and *either* she *or* her baby died as a result, God considered the guilty party a manslayer, and he had to pay "soul for soul."* (Exodus 21:22, 23) Imagine, then, how Jehovah must feel when he sees countless unborn babies deliberately aborted each year, many sacrificed on the altars of expediency and sexual liberation.

[17] What, though, about a woman who had an abortion prior to coming to a knowledge of Bible truth? Is she beyond God's mercy? Not at all! In fact, a truly repentant

---

* Bible lexicographers state that the wording of the Hebrew text "apparently renders it impracticable to refer the words to injury done to the woman alone." Note, too, that the Bible says nothing about the age of the embryo or fetus being a factor in Jehovah's judgment.

---

16. What Bible principle applies to abortion? (See also footnote.)
17. How would you comfort someone who had an abortion prior to learning about God's standards?

> ### DO I VIEW BLOOD AS SACRED?
>
> **Principle:** "Abstain from . . . blood."
> —Acts 15:20.
>
> **Some questions to ask yourself**
>
> ■ How would I describe the difference between the four primary components of blood and blood fractions?*
>
> ■ Why should I decide for myself whether I will accept or reject blood fractions or certain medical procedures involving the use of my own blood? —Romans 12:2; Galatians 6:5.
>
> ■ How would I explain to my physician why I accept or reject the use of blood fractions?—Proverbs 13:16.
>
> * See the Appendix, pages 215-16, for detailed information.

person can count on Jehovah's forgiveness based on Jesus' shed blood. (Psalm 103:8-14; Ephesians 1:7) Indeed, Christ himself said: "I have come to call, not righteous persons, but sinners to repentance."—Luke 5:32.

AVOID HURTFUL THINKING!

¹⁸ Beyond our simply not harming others, Jehovah wants us to root out of our heart the very cause of much bloodshed—hatred. "Everyone who hates his brother is a manslayer [or, murderer]," wrote the apostle John. (1 John 3:15) Such a person does not merely dislike his brother but wishes him dead. His enmity may surface in the form of vicious slander or false accusations that if true would merit divine judgment. (Leviticus 19:16; Deuteronomy 19:18-21; Matthew 5:22) How important, then, that we work at ridding our hearts of any ill will that may lodge there!—James 1:14, 15; 4:1-3.

¹⁹ Those who value life as Jehovah does and who want to keep themselves in his love also avoid violence in all its forms. Says Psalm 11:5: "Anyone loving violence [Jehovah's] soul certainly hates." That text is more than a statement about God's personality; it is a guiding principle for life. It moves lovers of God to avoid any form of entertainment that may foster a taste for violence. Likewise, the statement that Jehovah is "the God of peace" impels his servants to fill their minds and hearts with lovable, virtuous, and praiseworthy things, which make for peace. —Philippians 4:8, 9.

STAY CLEAR OF BLOODGUILTY ORGANIZATIONS

²⁰ In God's eyes, Satan's entire world is bloodguilty. Its political systems, portrayed in the Scriptures as vicious beasts, have slaughtered countless millions, includ-

---

18. How does the Bible address the underlying cause of much bloodshed?
19. How does a person who is governed by Bible principles view such texts as Psalm 11:5 and Philippians 4:8, 9?
20-22. What stand do Christians take toward the world, and why?

How would I explain to a physician my decision regarding the use of blood fractions?

ing many of Jehovah's servants. (Daniel 8:3, 4, 20-22; Revelation 13:1, 2, 7, 8) Hand in hand with these beastlike powers, business and science have worked to create some of the most heinous weapons imaginable, making huge profits in the process. How true that "the whole world is lying in the power of the wicked one"!—1 John 5:19.

21 Because Jesus' followers are "no part of the world" but remain strictly neutral toward its politics and wars, they avoid personal and community bloodguilt.* (John 15:19; 17:16) And in imitation of Christ, they do not respond violently when others persecute them. Rather, they show love for their enemies, even praying for them. —Matthew 5:44; Romans 12:17-21.

22 Above all, true Christians avoid involvement with "Babylon the Great," the world empire of false religion and the most bloodguilty of all. "In her," says God's

---

* See Chapter 5, "How to Keep Separate From the World."

Word, "was found the blood of prophets and of holy ones and of all those who have been slaughtered on the earth." Thus, we are warned: "Get out of her, my people."—Revelation 17:6; 18:2, 4, 24.

[23] Abandoning Babylon the Great involves more than having one's name removed from a membership roll. It also includes hating the evil practices that false religion condones or openly advocates—such things as immorality, political meddling, and the greedy pursuit of wealth. (Psalm 97:10; Revelation 18:7, 9, 11-17) How often these activities lead to bloodshed!

[24] Before taking up true worship, each of us, in one way or another, lent support to Satan's system and thus incurred a measure of bloodguilt. However, because we changed our ways, cultivated faith in Christ's ransom sacrifice, and dedicated our life to God, we gained God's mercy and spiritual protection. (Acts 3:19) That protection was prefigured in Bible times by the cities of refuge. —Numbers 35:11-15; Deuteronomy 21:1-9.

[25] How did that arrangement work? If an Israelite accidentally caused another's death, he was to flee to one of the cities of refuge. After qualified judges ruled on the matter, the accidental manslayer had to reside in the city of refuge until the death of the high priest. Then he would be free to live elsewhere. What a beautiful example of God's mercy and of the great value he places on human life! Corresponding today with those ancient cities of refuge is God's provision, based on Christ's ransom sacrifice, for protecting us from death for accidentally violating God's commandment about the sanctity of life and

---

23. What does it mean to get out of Babylon the Great?
24, 25. On what basis can God show mercy to a repentant person who is bloodguilty, and how was this prefigured in Bible times?

blood. Do you value that provision? How can you show that you do? One way is by inviting others to join you in the antitypical city of refuge, especially in view of the fast-approaching "great tribulation."—Matthew 24:21; 2 Corinthians 6:1, 2.

VALUE LIFE BY PREACHING THE KINGDOM MESSAGE

26 The situation of God's people in our day calls to mind that of the ancient prophet Ezekiel, whom Jehovah commissioned to serve as a spiritual watchman to the house of Israel. "You must hear [my] word and give them warning from me," said God. If Ezekiel were to neglect his commission, he would be held personally responsible for the blood of those executed when Jerusalem was called to account. (Ezekiel 33:7-9) But Ezekiel was obedient and incurred no bloodguilt.

27 Today, we face the end of Satan's entire world. Thus, Jehovah's Witnesses count it both an obligation and a privilege to proclaim God's "day of vengeance" in conjunction with the Kingdom message. (Isaiah 61:2; Matthew 24:14) Do you have a full share in this vital work? The apostle Paul took his preaching commission seriously. As a result, he could say: "I am clean from the blood of all men, for I have not held back from telling you all the counsel of God." (Acts 20:26, 27) What a fine example for us to imitate!

28 Of course, to keep ourselves in the warmth of Jehovah's fatherly love, we must do more than view life and blood as Jehovah does. We also need to remain clean, or holy, in his eyes, as we shall see in the following chapter.

26-28. In what way is our situation today similar to that of the prophet Ezekiel, and how can we keep ourselves in God's love?

CHAPTER 8

God Loves Clean People

"With the one keeping clean you will show yourself clean."—PSALM 18:26.

A MOTHER prepares her little boy to go out. She makes sure that he is bathed and that his clothes are neat and clean. She knows that good hygiene is crucial to his health. She also recognizes that her son's appearance reflects on his parents.

² Jehovah, our heavenly Father, wants his servants to be clean. His Word says: "With the one keeping clean you will show yourself clean."* (Psalm 18:26) Jehovah loves us; he knows that keeping clean is best for us. He also ex-

---

* The Hebrew word rendered "clean" describes not only physical cleanliness but also moral or spiritual cleanness.

1-3. (a) Why does a mother make sure that her son is neat and clean? (b) Why does Jehovah want his worshippers to be clean, and what motivates us to want to keep ourselves clean?

pects us as his Witnesses to reflect favorably on him. Indeed, our clean appearance and fine conduct will bring glory to, not reproach on, Jehovah and his holy name. —Ezekiel 36:22; 1 Peter 2:12.

³ Knowing that God loves clean people motivates us to keep clean. We want our way of life to bring honor to him because we love him. We also want to remain in his love. Let us, then, examine why we need to keep clean, what being clean involves, and how we can keep ourselves clean. Such an examination can help us to see whether there are areas in which we need to make improvement.

WHY DO WE NEED TO KEEP CLEAN?

⁴ One way Jehovah leads us is by example. His Word thus urges us to "become imitators of God." (Ephesians 5:1) Here is the primary reason why we need to keep clean: Jehovah, the God we worship, is clean, pure, and holy in every respect.—Leviticus 11:44, 45.

⁵ Jehovah's cleanness, like so many of his qualities and ways, is evident in his visible creations. (Romans 1:20) The earth was designed to be a clean home for humans. Jehovah has put into place ecological cycles that clean our air and water. Certain microbes act as a kind of sanitation department, transforming waste into harmless products. Scientists have utilized some of these hungry microorganisms to clean up oil spills and other pollution caused by human selfishness and greed. Obviously, cleanliness matters to "the Maker of the earth." (Jeremiah 10:12) It should also matter to us.

⁶ Another reason why we need to keep clean is that

4, 5. (a) What is the primary reason why we need to keep clean? (b) How is Jehovah's cleanness evident in his visible creations?
6, 7. How did the Mosaic Law emphasize that cleanness was required of those who worshipped Jehovah?

Jehovah, our Sovereign Ruler, requires cleanness of his worshippers. Under the Law that Jehovah gave to Israel, cleanness and worship were inseparable. The Law specified that on the Day of Atonement, the high priest had to bathe not once but twice. (Leviticus 16:4, 23, 24) Officiating priests were required to wash their hands and feet before offering sacrifices to Jehovah. (Exodus 30:17-21; 2 Chronicles 4:6) The Law outlined some 70 causes of physical uncleanness and ceremonial defilement. While in an unclean state, an Israelite could not have any part in worship—in certain cases, under penalty of death. (Leviticus 15:31) Anyone refusing to undergo the required purifying procedure, including bathing his body and washing his clothes, was to be "cut off from the midst of the congregation."—Numbers 19:17-20.

7 Although we are not under the Mosaic Law, it gives us insight into God's thinking on matters. Clearly, the Law emphasized that cleanness was required of those who worshipped God. Jehovah has not changed. (Malachi 3:6) Our worship cannot be acceptable to him unless it is "clean and undefiled." (James 1:27) We thus need to know what he expects of us in this regard.

WHAT BEING CLEAN IN GOD'S EYES INVOLVES

8 In the Bible, the idea of being clean means more than just physical cleanness. Being clean in God's eyes touches all aspects of our lives. Jehovah expects us to keep clean in four basic respects—spiritually, morally, mentally, and physically. Let us consider what each of these involves.

9 *Spiritual cleanness.* Put simply, keeping spiritually clean means not mixing true worship with false. When

---

8. In what respects does Jehovah expect us to keep clean?
9, 10. What does it mean to keep spiritually clean, and what do true Christians avoid?

the Israelites left Babylon to return to Jerusalem, they were to heed this inspired exhortation: "Get out of there, touch nothing unclean; . . . keep yourselves clean." (Isaiah 52:11) The Israelites were returning home primarily to restore Jehovah's worship. That worship had to be clean—not tainted by any of the God-dishonoring teachings, practices, and customs of Babylonish religion.

[10] Today, we as true Christians must be careful not to become contaminated by false worship. (1 Corinthians 10:21) Caution is essential in this regard, for the influence of false religion is pervasive. In many lands, various traditions, activities, and rituals are connected with false religious teachings, such as the notion that something inside us survives death. (Ecclesiastes 9:5, 6, 10) True Christians avoid customs involving false religious beliefs.[*] We will not allow pressure from others to cause us to compromise the Bible's standards of clean worship. —Acts 5:29.

[11] *Moral cleanness.* To keep morally clean includes avoiding sexual immorality of any kind. (Ephesians 5:5) It is vital that we stay morally clean. As we will see in the next chapter of this book, to remain in God's love, we must "flee from fornication." Unrepentant fornicators "will not inherit God's kingdom." (1 Corinthians 6:9, 10, 18) In God's eyes, such ones are among those who are "disgusting in their filth." If they fail to keep morally clean, "their portion will be . . . the second death."—Revelation 21:8.

---

[*] See Chapter 13 of this book for a discussion of specific celebrations and customs that true Christians avoid.

---

11. What does moral cleanness involve, and why is it vital that we keep clean in this respect?

¹² *Mental cleanness.* Thoughts lead to actions. If we allow wrong thoughts to take up residence in our mind and heart, sooner or later we are bound to commit unclean deeds. (Matthew 5:28; 15:18-20) But if we fill our mind with pure, clean thoughts, we can be motivated to maintain conduct that is clean. (Philippians 4:8) How can we keep mentally clean? For one thing, we need to avoid any form of entertainment that could soil our thinking.* In addition, we can fill our mind with clean thoughts by regularly studying God's Word.—Psalm 19:8, 9.

¹³ To remain in God's love, it is essential that we keep ourselves spiritually, morally, and mentally clean. These aspects of cleanness are discussed more fully in other chapters of this publication. Let us here examine the fourth aspect—*physical cleanliness.*

HOW CAN WE KEEP PHYSICALLY CLEAN?

¹⁴ Physical cleanliness involves keeping our body and surroundings clean. Is such cleanliness a personal matter that should be of no concern to anyone else? That could hardly be the case for worshippers of Jehovah. As already noted, our physical cleanliness matters to Jehovah not only because it is best for us but also because we reflect on him. Think about the illustration used at the outset. Seeing a child who is always dirty or unkempt makes you wonder about his parents, does it not? We would not want anything about our appearance or way of life to bring reproach on our heavenly Father or to detract from the message we preach. God's Word says: "In no way

---

* How to choose wholesome entertainment is considered in Chapter 6 of this publication.

12, 13. What connection is there between thoughts and actions, and how can we keep mentally clean?
14. Why is physical cleanliness not just a personal matter?

Physical cleanliness involves keeping our bodies and surroundings clean

are we giving any cause for stumbling, that our ministry might not be found fault with; but in every way we recommend ourselves as God's ministers." (2 Corinthians 6: 3, 4) How, then, can we keep physically clean?

15 *Our personal hygiene and appearance.* Although cultures and living conditions vary from country to country, we can generally find adequate soap and water to bathe regularly and to make sure that we and our children are clean. Good hygienic habits include washing our hands with soap and water before eating or handling food, after using the toilet, and after washing or changing a baby. Washing the hands with soap and water can prevent illness and actually save lives. It can prevent the

---

15, 16. What do good hygienic habits include, and what should be true of our clothing?

spread of harmful viruses and bacteria, thus helping people avoid diarrheic diseases. In lands where houses are not commonly connected to a sewage system, wastes can perhaps be disposed of by burying, as was done in ancient Israel.—Deuteronomy 23:12, 13.

¹⁶ Our clothing too requires regular washing to be clean and presentable. A Christian's clothing need not be expensive or the latest fashion, but it should be neat, clean, and modest. (1 Timothy 2:9, 10) No matter where we are, we want our appearance to "adorn the teaching of our Savior, God."—Titus 2:10.

¹⁷ *Our home and surroundings.* Our home may not be fancy or luxurious, but it should be as clean and presentable as circumstances permit. Likewise, if we use an automobile for transportation to meetings and in the field ministry, we can do our best to keep it reasonably clean, inside and out. Let us not forget that a clean home and surroundings are a witness in themselves. After all, we teach people that Jehovah is a clean God, that he will "bring to ruin those ruining the earth," and that his Kingdom will soon transform our earthly home into a paradise. (Revelation 11:18; Luke 23:43) Surely we want the appearance of our home and belongings to show others that even now we are developing clean habits that will fit in with the coming new world.

¹⁸ *Our place of worship.* Our love for Jehovah moves us to show respect for our Kingdom Hall, a center of true worship in the area. When new ones come to the hall, we want them to have a favorable impression of our meeting place. Regular cleaning and maintenance are needed in order to ensure that the hall remains appealing and at-

---

17. Why should our home and surroundings be clean and presentable?
18. How can we show respect for our Kingdom Hall?

tractive. We show respect for our Kingdom Hall by doing what we can to keep it in good condition. It is a privilege to volunteer our time to assist in cleaning and "mending and repairing" our place of worship. (2 Chronicles 34:10) The same principles apply when we meet at an Assembly Hall or another facility for assemblies or conventions.

CLEANSING OURSELVES OF DEFILING HABITS AND PRACTICES

[19] To keep ourselves physically clean, we need to avoid defiling habits and practices, such as smoking, abusing alcohol, and the nonmedical use of addictive or mind-altering substances. The Bible does not specifically name all the unclean and disgusting habits and practices that are prevalent today, but it does contain principles that enable us to perceive how Jehovah must feel about such things. Because we know Jehovah's view of matters, our love for him moves us to take the course that brings his approval. Let us consider five Scriptural principles.

[20] *"Since we have these promises, beloved ones, let us cleanse ourselves of every defilement of flesh and spirit, perfecting holiness in God's fear."* (2 Corinthians 7:1) Jehovah wants us to be free of practices that pollute our fleshly body and damage our spirit, or dominant mental inclination. We must therefore avoid addictive behaviors that are known to be harmful to physical and mental health.

[21] The Bible gives a powerful reason for us to "cleanse ourselves of every defilement." Notice that 2 Corinthians 7:1 begins by saying: "Since we have these promises." What promises? As mentioned in the preceding verses, Jehovah promises: "I will take you in. And I shall be a

---

19. To keep ourselves physically clean, what do we need to avoid, and how does the Bible help us in this regard?
20, 21. Jehovah wants us to be free of what type of practices, and what powerful reason do we have to comply?

DO I FIGHT TO DO WHAT IS RIGHT?

Principle: "I pummel my body and lead it as a slave, that, after I have preached to others, I myself should not become disapproved somehow." —1 Corinthians 9:27.

Some questions to ask yourself

- When I first feel the urge to engage in some defiling habit, do I pray for God's spirit to help me resist the impulse?—Matthew 6:13.

- How do the people I associate with, the movies I watch, and the music I listen to affect my determination to remain free from bad habits? —1 Peter 4:3, 4.

- Why does performing good works not justify sinful conduct?—Matthew 23:25-28.

- Why am I willing to suffer in the same way that Jesus suffered for doing God's will?—1 Peter 2:21; 4:1.

- How would I explain to someone why I choose not to smoke?—Romans 12:1, 2.

- Do I realize that having a relapse with regard to some unclean practice does not mean that I am a complete failure? —Romans 7:21-25.

father to you." (2 Corinthians 6:17, 18) Just imagine: Jehovah promises to put you under his protective care and to love you as a father does a son or a daughter. But Jehovah will fulfill these promises only if you avoid defilements of "flesh and spirit." How foolish it would be, then, to allow any disgusting habit or practice to rob you of such a precious and close relationship with Jehovah!

22 *"You must love Jehovah your God with your whole heart and with your whole soul and with your whole mind."* (Matthew 22:37) Jesus singled out this commandment as the greatest of all. (Matthew 22:38) Jehovah deserves such love from us. To love him with our whole heart, soul, and mind, we must avoid practices that could shorten our life or dull our God-given thinking abilities.

23 *"[Jehovah] gives to all persons life and breath and all things."* (Acts 17:24, 25) Life is a gift from God. We love the Giver, so we want to show respect for the gift. We shun any habits or practices that are detrimental to our health, for we recognize that such practices show a gross disrespect for the gift of life.—Psalm 36:9.

24 *"You must love your neighbor as yourself."* (Matthew 22:39) Unclean habits and practices often affect not only the practicer but also those around him. For example, exposure to secondhand smoke can have a harmful effect on nonsmokers. An individual who hurts those around him is violating the divine requirement that we love our neighbor. He also belies any claim that he loves God. —1 John 4:20, 21.

25 *"Be in subjection and be obedient to governments and authorities as rulers."* (Titus 3:1) In many lands, the possession or use of certain drugs is a violation of the law.

22-25. What Scriptural principles can help us to avoid unclean habits and practices?

> ### "WITH GOD ALL THINGS ARE POSSIBLE"
>
> "At age 15," says Helen,* "I was smoking cigarettes every day and drinking alcohol with my friends on weekends. Later, although I was now a single mother with three children, I became addicted to crack cocaine. My life was a mess. However, I started studying the Bible, and with Jehovah's help, I cleaned up my life and broke free from my addictions. It was a real struggle, especially to give up using cocaine. I think it would have been impossible for me to make these changes on my own. But now I can truly say that in my life, I have seen proof of Jesus' words: 'With God all things are possible.'"—Matthew 19:26.
>
> ---
>
> * Name has been changed.

As true Christians, we do not possess or use illegal drugs. —Romans 13:1.

26 To remain in God's love, we need to keep clean, not just in one or two respects but in all respects. Abandoning and keeping clear of defiling habits and practices may not be easy, but it is possible.* Really, there is no better way to live, for Jehovah always teaches us to benefit ourselves. (Isaiah 48:17) Most important, by keeping clean we can have the satisfaction that comes from knowing that we are reflecting favorably on the God we love, thereby remaining in his love.

---

* See the boxes "Do I Fight to Do What Is Right?" on page 94, and "With God All Things Are Possible," above.

---

26. (a) To remain in God's love, what do we need to do? (b) Why is keeping clean in God's eyes the best way to live?

CHAPTER 9

"Flee From Fornication"

"Deaden, therefore, your body members that are upon the earth as respects fornication, uncleanness, sexual appetite, hurtful desire, and covetousness, which is idolatry."—COLOSSIANS 3:5.

THE fisherman goes down to his favorite spot. He has a particular kind of fish in mind. He selects a lure and casts his line into the water. Moments later, the line goes taut, the rod bends, and he reels in his catch. Smiling, he knows he has chosen the right lure.

² In the year 1473 B.C.E., a man named Balaam gave much thought to a lure. His intended prey, though, were God's people, who were camped on the Plains of Moab, at the border of the Promised Land. Balaam professed to be a prophet of Jehovah, but he was really just a greedy man hired to curse Israel. However, through Jehovah's intervention, Balaam was only able to bless Israel. Set on earning his reward, Balaam reasoned that perhaps he could induce God to curse his own people, if only they could be tempted to commit gross sin. With that goal in mind, Balaam cast the lure—the seductive young women of Moab.—Numbers 22:1-7; 31:15, 16; Revelation 2:14.

³ Did this strategy work? To an extent, yes. Tens of thousands of Israelite men took the lure by having "immoral relations with the daughters of Moab."

1, 2. How did Balaam scheme to cause harm to Jehovah's people?
3. To what extent did Balaam's scheme succeed?

They even began to worship Moabite gods, including the disgusting Baal of Peor, a god of fertility, or sex. As a result, 24,000 Israelites perished right at the border of the Promised Land. What a monumental tragedy that was!—Numbers 25:1-9.

⁴ What paved the way for this calamity? Many of the people had developed a wicked heart by drawing away from Jehovah, the very God who had delivered them from Egypt, fed them in the wilderness, and led them safely to the land of promise. (Hebrews 3:12) Reflecting on the matter, the apostle Paul wrote: "Neither let us practice fornication, as some of them committed fornication, only to fall, twenty-three thousand of them in one day."*—1 Corinthians 10:8.

⁵ The account in Numbers has many important lessons for God's people today, who stand at the thresh-

---

* The figure given in Numbers evidently included "the head ones of the people" executed by the judges, which may have amounted to 1,000 men, and those executed directly by Jehovah.—Numbers 25:4, 5.

---

4. Why did thousands of Israelites fall prey to immorality?
5, 6. Why is the account about Israel's sin on the Plains of Moab valuable to us today?

Looking across the Plains of Moab

old of a far greater promised land. (1 Corinthians 10:11) For example, the world's obsession with sex reflects that of the ancient Moabites but on a larger scale. Moreover, each year thousands of Christians fall prey to immorality—the same basic lure that caught the Israelites. (2 Corinthians 2:11) And in imitation of Zimri, who boldly paraded a Midianite woman right into the Israelite camp to his own tent, some who associate with God's people today have become a corrupting influence within the Christian congregation.—Numbers 25:6, 14; Jude 4.

⁶ Do you see yourself on the modern-day Plains of Moab? Can you see your prize—the long-awaited new world—on the horizon? If so, then do everything in your power to remain in God's love by heeding the command: "Flee from fornication."—1 Corinthians 6:18.

WHAT IS FORNICATION?

⁷ As used in the Bible, "fornication" (Greek, *por·nei′a*) applies to illicit sexual relations outside of Scriptural marriage. It includes adultery, prostitution, and sex relations between unmarried individuals, as well as oral and anal sex and the sexual manipulation of the genitals of an individual to whom one is not married. It also includes such acts between individuals of the same sex as well as bestiality.*

⁸ The Scriptures are very clear: Those who practice fornication cannot remain in the Christian congregation and will not receive everlasting life. (1 Corinthians 6:9;

---

* For a discussion of the meaning of uncleanness and loose conduct, see "Questions From Readers" in *The Watchtower* of July 15, 2006, published by Jehovah's Witnesses.

7, 8. What is "fornication," and how do those who practice it reap what they sow?

Revelation 22:15) What is more, even now they bring much harm to themselves in the form of a loss of trust and self-respect, marital discord, a guilty conscience, unwanted pregnancies, disease, and even death. (Galatians 6:7, 8) Why start down a path that is littered with so much misery? Sadly, many do not think that far ahead when they take the first wrong step—which quite often involves pornography.

PORNOGRAPHY—A FIRST STEP

9 In many lands, pornography is featured on newsstands, in music, and on television, and it virtually saturates the Internet.* Is it harmless, as some claim? Absolutely not! Those who view pornography may become habitual masturbators and nurture "disgraceful sexual appetites," which may result in an addiction to sex, perverted desires, serious marital disharmony, and even divorce.# (Romans 1:24-27; Ephesians 4:19) A researcher likens sex addiction to cancer. "It keeps growing and spreading," he says. "It rarely ever reverses itself, and it is also very difficult to treat and heal."

10 Consider the words recorded at James 1:14, 15, which reads: "Each one is tried by being drawn out and enticed by his own desire. Then the desire, when it has become fertile, gives birth to sin; in turn, sin, when it

---

* "Pornography," as used here, refers to the depiction in pictures, in writing, or by voice of erotic material that is intended to cause sexual excitement. Pornography may range from a picture of a person in an erotic pose to depictions of sexual acts of the most sordid kind between two or more individuals.

Masturbation is discussed in the Appendix, pages 218-19.

---

9. Is pornography harmless, as some claim? Explain.
10. In what ways can we apply the principle found at James 1:14, 15? (See also the box on page 101.)

has been accomplished, brings forth death." So if a bad desire enters your mind, take immediate action to get rid of it! For example, if you inadvertently see erotic images, quickly look away, or turn off the computer, or change the TV channel. Do whatever is necessary to avoid succumbing to immoral desire before it races out of control and overcomes you!—Matthew 5:29, 30.

[11] For good reason, the One who knows us better than we know ourselves exhorts: "Deaden, therefore, your body members that are upon the earth as respects fornication, uncleanness, sexual appetite, hurtful desire, and

---

11. When fighting wrong desires, how can we demonstrate our trust in Jehovah?

FINDING THE STRENGTH TO BE MORALLY CLEAN

"While in my teens, I became trapped in a cycle of viewing pornography and masturbating," says a young man. "My peers at school considered such conduct a normal part of adolescence. But it damaged my conscience, and I was drawn into a life of immorality. I eventually realized that I was just a slave to my desires. However, I was able to overcome my unclean habits with help from Jehovah and the congregation. Now I am careful about whom I associate with, since I know that others can have a big influence on me. I have found that regular prayer and personal Bible study are essential to keep me from falling back into bad habits. Instead of being a slave to fleshly desires, I now have the privilege of serving as a regular pioneer."

covetousness, which is idolatry." (Colossians 3:5) True, doing so may be a challenge. But remember, we have a loving and patient heavenly Father to call upon. (Psalm 68:19) So turn quickly to him when wrong thoughts enter your mind. Pray for "power beyond what is normal," and force your mind to focus on other matters.—2 Corinthians 4:7; 1 Corinthians 9:27; see the box "How Can I Break a Bad Habit?" on page 104.

[12] The wise man Solomon wrote: "More than all else that is to be guarded, safeguard your heart, for out of it are the sources of life." (Proverbs 4:23) Our "heart" is our inner self, what we really are as a person in God's eyes. Moreover, it is God's estimation of our "heart" —not what we may appear to be in the eyes of others—that determines whether we receive everlasting life or not. It is that simple. It is also that serious. So that he would not look indecently at a woman, faithful Job made a covenant, or formal agreement, with his eyes. (Job 31:1) What a fine example for us! Showing the same mind, a psalmist prayed: "Make my eyes pass on from seeing what is worthless."—Psalm 119:37.

DINAH'S UNWISE CHOICE

[13] As we saw in Chapter 3, our friends can exert a powerful influence on us for good or for bad. (Proverbs 13:20; 1 Corinthians 15:33) Consider the example of Dinah, a daughter of the patriarch Jacob. (Genesis 34:1) Despite her good upbringing, Dinah unwisely made friends with Canaanite girls. Like the Moabites, the Canaanites were notoriously immoral. (Leviticus 18:6-25) In the eyes of Canaanite men, including Shechem—"the most honor-

---

12. What is our "heart," and why must we safeguard it?
13. Who was Dinah, and why was her choice of friends unwise?

Restricting Internet use to a public area of the home is the course of wisdom

able" of his father's household—Dinah seemed to be legitimate prey.—Genesis 34:18, 19.

¹⁴ Dinah probably did not have sexual relations in mind when she saw Shechem. He, though, did what most Canaanites would have considered natural when sexually aroused. Any last-minute resistance on Dinah's part meant little, for he "took her" and "violated her." It seems that Shechem later "fell in love" with Dinah, but that did not change what he had done to her. (Genesis 34:1-4) And Dinah was not the only one to suffer as a result. Her choice of associates triggered events that brought disgrace and reproach on her whole family. —Genesis 34:7, 25-31; Galatians 6:7, 8.

¹⁵ If Dinah learned an important lesson, she learned it

---

14. How did Dinah's choice of friends lead to tragedy?
15, 16. How can we gain true wisdom? (See also the box on page 109.)

> ## HOW CAN I BREAK A BAD HABIT?
>
> **Principle:** "O you lovers of Jehovah, hate what is bad."—Psalm 97:10.
>
> ### Some questions to ask yourself
>
> - Am I avoiding situations that might stimulate wrong desires?—Matthew 5:27, 28.
>
> - Do I meditate on the consequences of acting on wrong desires?—Proverbs 22:3.
>
> - What type of decisive action am I willing to take to overcome my bad habit?—Matthew 5:29, 30.
>
> - Am I prepared to talk to a parent or a spiritually mature friend about my problem?—Proverbs 1:8, 9; Galatians 6:1, 2.
>
> - How can I demonstrate that I rely on Jehovah's strength and wisdom to gain the victory? —Proverbs 3:5, 6; James 1:5.

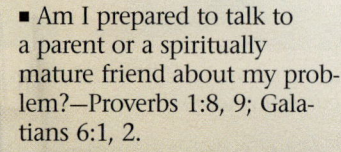

the hard way. Those who love and obey Jehovah do not have to learn life's lessons the hard way. Because they listen to God, they choose to 'walk with wise persons.' (Proverbs 13:20a) Thus they come to understand "the entire course of what is good" and avoid needless problems and pains.—Proverbs 2:6-9; Psalm 1:1-3.

[16] Godly wisdom is available to all who yearn for it and

who act on that yearning by persisting in prayer and by regularly studying God's Word and the material provided by the faithful slave class. (Matthew 24:45; James 1:5) Also important is humility, which is reflected in a willingness to heed Scriptural counsel. (2 Kings 22:18, 19) For example, a Christian may accept in principle that his heart can be treacherous and desperate. (Jeremiah 17:9) But when the situation calls for it, is he humble enough to accept specific, loving counsel and help?

¹⁷ Imagine this situation. A father does not allow his daughter and a young Christian man to go out unchaperoned. The girl responds: "But Dad, don't you trust me? We won't do anything wrong!" She may love Jehovah and have the best of intentions, yet is she "walking in [godly] wisdom"? Is she 'fleeing from fornication'? Or is she foolishly "trusting in [her] own heart"? (Proverbs 28:26) Perhaps you can think of additional principles that would assist such a father and his daughter in reasoning on the matter.—See Proverbs 22:3; Matthew 6: 13; 26:41.

JOSEPH FLED FROM FORNICATION

¹⁸ A fine young person who loved God and fled from fornication was Joseph, Dinah's half brother. (Genesis 30:20-24) As a child, Joseph saw firsthand the fruits of his sister's folly. No doubt these memories, as well as Joseph's desire to remain in God's love, protected him years later in Egypt when his master's wife tried to seduce him "day after day." Of course, as a slave Joseph could not simply hand in his resignation and leave! He had to deal

---

17. Describe a situation that may arise within a family, and show how a father might reason with his daughter.
18, 19. What temptation arose in Joseph's life, and how did he deal with it?

with the situation wisely and courageously. This he did by repeatedly saying no to Potiphar's wife and, in the end, by fleeing from her.—Genesis 39:7-12.

¹⁹ Consider: If Joseph had fantasized about the woman or had habitually daydreamed about sex, would he have been able to keep his integrity? Most likely not. Instead of entertaining sinful thoughts, Joseph prized his relationship with Jehovah, which was evident in his words to Potiphar's wife. "My master," he would say, "has not withheld from me anything at all except you, because you are his wife. So how could I commit this great badness and actually sin against God?"—Genesis 39:8, 9.

²⁰ Imagine the joy that Jehovah must have felt as he observed young Joseph, far from his family, maintaining his integrity day after day. (Proverbs 27:11) Later, Jehovah maneuvered matters so that Joseph was not only released from prison but also made Egypt's prime minister and food administrator! (Genesis 41:39-49) How true the words of Psalm 97:10: "O you lovers of Jehovah, hate what is bad. He is guarding the souls of his loyal ones; out of the hand of the wicked ones he delivers them"!

20. How did Jehovah maneuver matters in the case of Joseph?

21 Likewise today, many servants of God demonstrate that they "hate what is bad, and love what is good." (Amos 5:15) A young brother in an African land recalls that a female classmate boldly offered him sex in exchange for his help during a mathematics test. "I immediately rejected her offer," he says. "By maintaining integrity, I have kept my dignity and self-respect, which are far more valuable than gold and silver." True, sin may give "temporary enjoyment," but such cheap thrills often bring much pain. (Hebrews 11:25) Moreover, they pale into insignificance when compared with the lasting happiness that results from obedience to Jehovah.—Proverbs 10:22.

ACCEPT HELP FROM THE GOD OF MERCY

22 Being imperfect, we all struggle to subdue fleshly desires and do what is right in God's eyes. (Romans 7:21-25) Jehovah is aware of this, "remembering that we are dust." (Psalm 103:14) Sometimes, though, a Christian may commit a serious sin. Is his situation hopeless? By no means! Granted, the wrongdoer may reap bitter fruitage, as did King David. Nevertheless, God is always "ready to forgive" those who are contrite and "openly confess" their sins.—Psalm 86:5; James 5:16; Proverbs 28:13.

23 In addition, God has kindly provided the Christian congregation with "gifts in men"—mature spiritual shepherds who are both qualified and eager to render help. (Ephesians 4:8, 12; James 5:14, 15) Their goal is to assist a wrongdoer in restoring his relationship with God and, in the words of the wise man, in "acquiring heart" so that he does not repeat the sin.—Proverbs 15:32.

---

21. How did a young brother in an African land show moral courage?
22, 23. (a) If a Christian commits a serious sin, why is his situation not hopeless? (b) What help is available to a wrongdoer?

'ACQUIRE HEART'

24 The Bible speaks of people "in want of heart" and of those "acquiring heart." (Proverbs 7:7) Because of spiritual immaturity and inexperience in God's service, someone "in want of heart" may lack discernment and good judgment. Like the young man described at Proverbs 7:6-23, he may more readily fall victim to serious sin. However, "he that is acquiring heart" gives serious attention to the inner person by means of regular, prayerful study of God's Word. And to the extent possible in his imperfect state, he harmonizes his thoughts, desires, emotions, and goals in life with what God approves. Thus he is "loving his own soul," or blessing himself, and "is going to find good."—Proverbs 19:8.

25 Ask yourself: 'Am I fully convinced that God's standards are right? Do I firmly believe that adherence to them results in the greatest happiness?' (Psalm 19:7-10; Isaiah 48:17, 18) If you have even a tiny doubt, address the situation. Meditate on the consequences of ignoring God's laws. In addition, "taste and see that Jehovah is good" by living the truth and by filling your mind with wholesome thoughts—things that are true, righteous, chaste, lovable, and virtuous. (Psalm 34:8; Philippians 4:8, 9) You can be sure, the more you do so, the more you grow to love God, to love what he loves, and to hate what he hates. Joseph was no superman. Yet, he was able to "flee from fornication" because he allowed Jehovah to mold him over many years, to give him heart. May the same be true of you.—Isaiah 64:8.

24, 25. (a) How did the young man described at Proverbs 7:6-23 show that he was "in want of heart"? (b) How can we 'acquire heart'?

> ## SCRIPTURES FOR MEDITATION
>
> "O you lovers of Jehovah, hate what is bad."
> —Psalm 97:10.
>
> "Everyone that keeps on looking at a woman so as to have a passion for her has already committed adultery with her in his heart."—Matthew 5:28.
>
> "He that practices fornication is sinning against his own body."—1 Corinthians 6:18.
>
> "I pummel my body and lead it as a slave, that, after I have preached to others, I myself should not become disapproved somehow."
> —1 Corinthians 9:27.
>
> "Whatever a man is sowing, this he will also reap; because he who is sowing with a view to his flesh will reap corruption from his flesh, but he who is sowing with a view to the spirit will reap everlasting life from the spirit."—Galatians 6:7, 8.
>
> "Deaden, therefore, your body members that are upon the earth as respects fornication, uncleanness, sexual appetite."—Colossians 3:5.
>
> "Each one of you should know how to get possession of his own vessel in sanctification and honor, not in covetous sexual appetite."
> —1 Thessalonians 4:4, 5.

[26] Our Creator formed our reproductive organs, not to be toys for mere thrills, but to enable us to reproduce and to enjoy intimacy within marriage. (Proverbs 5:18) God's view of marriage will be discussed in the following two chapters.

---
26. What important topic will be considered next?

CHAPTER 10

Marriage—A Gift From a Loving God

"A threefold cord cannot quickly be torn."
—ECCLESIASTES 4:12.

DO YOU enjoy going to weddings? Many do, for such occasions can be very pleasant. You see the couple looking their best. Better yet, there is such joy on their faces! On this day, they are all smiles, and their future seems full of hope and promise.

² Still, it must be admitted that in many respects the institution of marriage is in a shambles today. While we hope for the best for newly married couples, we may at times wonder: 'Will this marriage be happy? Will it last?' The answers to those questions will depend on whether husband and wife trust and apply God's counsel on marriage. (Proverbs 3:5, 6) They need to do so in order to remain in God's love. Let us now focus on the Bible's answer to these four questions: Why get married? If you marry, whom should you choose for a mate? How can you prepare for marriage? And what can help a couple to remain happily married?

WHY GET MARRIED?

³ Some believe that marriage is essential to happiness —that you cannot find fulfillment or joy in life unless you find a mate. That is simply untrue! Jesus, a single

---

1, 2. (a) Regarding new marriages, what may we at times wonder, and why? (b) What questions will we discuss in this chapter?
3. Why would it be unwise to marry for trivial reasons?

man, spoke of singleness as a gift and urged those who could to make room for it. (Matthew 19:11, 12) The apostle Paul too discussed the advantages of singleness. (1 Corinthians 7:32-38) Neither Jesus nor Paul made a rule in this regard; in fact, "forbidding to marry" is listed among "teachings of demons." (1 Timothy 4:1-3) Still, singleness has much to offer those who want to serve Jehovah without distraction. It would not be wise, then, to marry for trivial reasons, such as peer pressure.

4 On the other hand, are there valid reasons to get married? Yes. Marriage too is a gift from our loving God. (Genesis 2:18) So it has certain advantages and the potential for bringing blessings. For instance, a good marriage is the best foundation for family life. Children need a stable environment with parents to raise them, providing love, discipline, and guidance. (Psalm 127:3; Ephesians 6:1-4) However, child-rearing is not the only reason for marriage.

5 Consider the theme scripture for this chapter along with its context: "Two are better than one, because they have a good reward for their hard work. For if one of them should fall, the other one can raise his partner up. But how will it be with just the one who falls when there is not another to raise him up? Moreover, if two lie down together, they also will certainly get warm; but how can just one keep warm? And if somebody could overpower one alone, two together could make a stand against him. And a threefold cord cannot quickly be torn in two." —Ecclesiastes 4:9-12.

---

4. A good marriage provides what foundation for child-rearing?
5, 6. (a) According to Ecclesiastes 4:9-12, what are some of the practical benefits of a close friendship? (b) How can a marriage be like a threefold cord?

⁶ Primarily, this passage is about the value of friendship. Marriage, of course, involves the closest of friendships. As this scripture shows, such a union can provide assistance, comfort, and protection. A marriage is especially strong if it is more than a bond between just two people. A twofold cord, as this verse implies, might be torn apart. But three strands woven or braided together would be much harder to tear apart. When pleasing Jehovah is the prime concern of both husband and wife, their marriage is like that threefold cord. Jehovah is a real part of the marriage, so the union is very strong indeed.

⁷ Marriage is also the only context in which sexual desires can be properly satisfied. In this setting, the sexual union is rightly viewed as a source of delight. (Proverbs 5:18) When a single person is past what the Bible calls "the bloom of youth"—that time when sexual urges first become strong—he or she may still struggle with sexual desires. Uncontrolled, such desires could lead to unclean or improper conduct. Paul was inspired to pen this counsel for single people: "If they do not have self-control, let them marry, for it is better to marry than to be inflamed with passion."—1 Corinthians 7:9, 36; James 1:15.

⁸ Whatever reasons motivate a person to marry, it is good to be realistic. As Paul put it, those who marry "will have tribulation in their flesh." (1 Corinthians 7:28) Married people face challenges that single people will not face. If you choose to marry, though, how can you minimize the challenges and maximize the blessings? One way is to choose a mate wisely.

7, 8. (a) What counsel did Paul pen for single Christians who struggle with sexual desires? (b) The Bible gives us what realistic view of marriage?

WHO WOULD MAKE A GOOD MARRIAGE MATE?

⁹ Paul was inspired to write down a vital principle that should be applied when choosing a marriage mate: "Do not become unevenly yoked with unbelievers." (2 Corinthians 6:14) His illustration was based on a fact of agricultural life. If two animals that differ greatly in size or strength are yoked together, both will suffer. Similarly, yoked together by marriage, a believer and an unbeliever will undoubtedly face friction and strains. If one mate wants to remain in Jehovah's love and the other cares little or nothing about that, their priorities in life will not match, and much discomfort is likely to result. Paul thus urged Christians to marry "only in the Lord."—1 Corinthians 7:39.

¹⁰ In some cases, single Christians have come to the conclusion that an uneven yoking would be better than the loneliness they currently feel. Some decide to ignore Bible counsel, and they marry a person who does not serve Jehovah. Again and again, the outcome is sad. Such ones find themselves married to a person with whom they cannot share the most important things in life. The loneliness that results may be far greater than any that they experienced before they married. Happily, there are many thousands of single Christians who trust in and loyally adhere to divine counsel in this regard. (Psalm 32:8) Though hoping to marry someday, they remain single until they find a mate among those who worship Jehovah God.

¹¹ Of course, not every servant of Jehovah is

9, 10. (a) How did Paul illustrate the danger of forming close bonds with unbelievers? (b) What often results from ignoring God's counsel not to marry an unbeliever?

11. What can help you to choose a marriage mate wisely? (See also the box on page 114.)

WHAT AM I LOOKING FOR IN A MATE?

Principle: "The two will be one flesh.
—Matthew 19:5.

Some questions to ask yourself

■ Why is it important to be "past the bloom of youth" before marrying?—1 Corinthians 7:36; 13:11; Matthew 19:4, 5.

■ Although I am old enough to marry, how can I benefit from staying single for a period of time?
—1 Corinthians 7:32-34, 37, 38.

■ If I choose to marry, why is it important that my prospective mate have a record of faithful service to Jehovah?
—1 Corinthians 7:39.

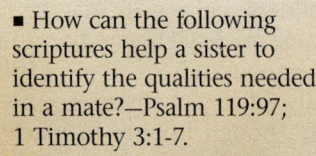

■ How can the following scriptures help a sister to identify the qualities needed in a mate?—Psalm 119:97; 1 Timothy 3:1-7.

■ How could Proverbs 31:10-31 help a brother choose a marriage mate wisely?

automatically a suitable marriage mate. If you are considering marriage, look for someone whose personality, spiritual goals, and love for God are compatible with your own. The faithful slave class has provided much food for thought on this subject, and you would do well to consider such Scriptural counsel prayerfully, letting it guide you in making this important decision.*—Psalm 119:105.

[12] In many lands, it is customary for parents to choose a mate for their child. It is widely agreed in those cultures that parents have the greater wisdom and experience needed to make such an important choice. Arranged marriages often work out well, as they did in Bible times. The example of Abraham sending his servant to find a wife for Isaac is instructive to parents who may be in a similar position today. Money and social standing were not Abraham's concern. Rather, he went to great lengths to find a wife for Isaac among people who worshipped Jehovah.#—Genesis 24:3, 67.

HOW CAN YOU PREPARE FOR A SUCCESSFUL MARRIAGE?

[13] If you are thinking seriously about marriage, you would do well to ask yourself, 'Am I really ready?' The

---

* See chapter 2 of *The Secret of Family Happiness*, published by Jehovah's Witnesses.

Some faithful patriarchs had more than one wife. When Jehovah dealt with the patriarchs and with fleshly Israel, he tolerated the practice of polygamy. He did not institute it, but he did regulate it. However, Christians keep in mind that Jehovah no longer allows polygamy among his worshippers.—Matthew 19:9; 1 Timothy 3:2.

---

12. What custom regarding marriage prevails in many lands, and what Bible example offers some guidance?
13-15. (a) How can the principle found at Proverbs 24:27 help a young man who is thinking about marriage? (b) What can a young woman do to prepare for marriage?

answer does not simply lie in your feelings about love, sex, companionship, or child rearing. Rather, there are specific goals that each prospective husband or wife should think about.

[14] A young man who seeks a wife should think carefully about this principle: "Prepare your work out of doors, and make it ready for yourself in the field. Afterward you must also build up your household." (Proverbs 24:27) What is the point? In those days, if a man wanted to "build up [his] household," or establish a family by getting married, he needed to ask himself, 'Am I ready to care for and support a wife and any children who might come along?' He had to work first, caring for his fields, or crops. The same principle applies today. A man who wants to marry needs to prepare for the responsibility. As long as he is physically able, he will have to work. God's Word indicates that a man who does not care for the physical, emotional, and spiritual needs of his family is worse than one without faith!—1 Timothy 5:8.

[15] A woman who decides to marry is likewise agreeing to shoulder a number of weighty responsibilities. The Bible praises some of the skills and qualities that a wife may need as she helps her husband and cares for her household. (Proverbs 31:10-31) Men and women who rush into marriage without preparing to take on the responsibilities involved are really being selfish, failing to think of what they can offer a potential mate. Most of all, though, those contemplating marriage need to be prepared spiritually.

[16] Preparing for marriage involves meditating on the roles that God has assigned to husband and wife. A man

---

16, 17. Those preparing for marriage should meditate on what Scriptural principles?

needs to know what it means to be the head of a Christian household. This role is not a license to act as a tyrant. Rather, he must imitate the manner in which Jesus exercises headship. (Ephesians 5:23) Likewise, a Christian woman needs to understand the dignified role of the wife. Will she be willing to submit to "the law of her husband"? (Romans 7:2) She is already under the law of Jehovah and of Christ. (Galatians 6:2) Her husband's authority in the household represents another law. Can she be supportive and submissive when it comes to the authority of an imperfect man? If that prospect is not appealing, she does well to refrain from marrying.

¹⁷ Further, each mate needs to be ready to care for the special needs of the other. (Philippians 2:4) Paul wrote: "Let each one of you individually so love his wife as he does himself; on the other hand, the wife should have deep respect for her husband." Under divine inspiration, Paul saw that the man has a special need to sense his wife's deep respect for him. And the woman has a special need to feel loved by her husband.—Ephesians 5: 21-33.

¹⁸ Courtship, then, is not merely a time to have fun. It is a time for a man and a woman to learn how to deal properly with each other, to see whether marriage would be a wise choice. It is also a time to exercise self-control! The temptation to become physically intimate can be very strong—after all, the attraction is natural. However, those who truly love each other will avoid any acts that could harm a loved one spiritually. (1 Thessalonians 4:6) So if you are courting, exercise self-control; you can benefit from that quality throughout your life, whether you marry or not.

---

18. Why should couples exercise self-control during courtship?

HOW CAN YOU MAKE A MARRIAGE LAST?

[19] If a couple is to make their marriage last, they need to have the right view of commitment. In novels and movies, a marriage often provides the happy ending that people crave. In real life, though, marriage is not an ending; it is a beginning—the start of something that Jehovah designed to last. (Genesis 2:24) Sadly, that is not the common view in today's world. In some cultures, people speak of marrying as "tying the knot." They may not realize how aptly that illustration describes the common view of marriage. How so? While a good knot should hold fast as long as it is needed, another key requirement is that it can be tied and *untied* with ease.

[20] Many today see marriage as temporary. They enter into it readily enough because they think that it will suit their needs, but they expect to be able to get out of it as soon as it seems to be challenging. Remember, though, the illustration that the Bible uses for a bond such as marriage—the cord. Cords or ropes made for sailing ships are designed to last, never to fray or unravel, even in the harshest storm. Likewise, marriage is designed to endure. Remember, Jesus said: "What God has yoked together let no man put apart." (Matthew 19:6) If you marry, you need to have the same view of marriage. Does that kind of commitment turn marriage into a burden? No.

[21] A husband and wife need to maintain the right view of each other. If each one strives to focus on the good

---

19, 20. How should a Christian's view of marriage differ from that of many in today's world? Illustrate.

21. A husband and wife need to maintain what attitude toward each other, and what may help them to do so?

qualities and efforts of the other, the marriage will be a source of joy and refreshment. Is it unrealistic to have such a positive view of an imperfect mate? Jehovah is never unrealistic, yet we count on him to maintain a positive view of us. The psalmist asked: "If errors were what you watch, O Jah, O Jehovah, who could stand?" (Psalm 130:3) Husbands and wives need to have a similarly positive and forgiving view of each other.—Colossians 3:13.

During courtship, many couples wisely arrange for a chaperone

²² Marriage can become a greater blessing as it endures over the years. The Bible shows us the marriage of Abraham and Sarah when they were an elderly couple. Their life was by no means free of hardships and challenges. Imagine what it was like for Sarah, a woman possibly in her 60's, to leave her comfortable home in the prosperous city of Ur and take up dwelling in tents for the rest of her life. Yet, she submitted to her husband's headship. A true complement and helper to Abraham, she respectfully helped to make his decisions work. And her subjection was not superficial. Even "inside herself," she referred to her husband as her lord. (Genesis 18:12; 1 Peter 3:6) Her respect for Abraham came from the heart.

²³ Of course, that does not mean that Abraham and Sarah always saw things the same way. She once made a suggestion that was "very displeasing" to Abraham. Still, at Jehovah's direction, Abraham humbly listened to the voice of his wife, which turned out to be a blessing to the family. (Genesis 21:9-13) Husbands and wives today, even those married for decades, can learn much from this godly couple.

²⁴ In the Christian congregation, there are many thousands of happy marriages—marriages in which the wife deeply respects her husband, the husband loves and honors his wife, and both work together to put the doing of Jehovah's will first in all things. If you decide to marry, may you choose your mate wisely, prepare well for marriage, and work at a peaceful, loving marriage that brings honor to Jehovah God. In that case, your marriage will certainly help you to remain in God's love.

22, 23. How did Abraham and Sarah set a good example for married people today?
24. What kind of marriages reflect well on Jehovah God, and why?

Chapter 11

"Let Marriage Be Honorable"

"Rejoice with the wife of your youth."
—PROVERBS 5:18.

ARE you married? If so, is your marriage a source of happiness, or are you experiencing serious marital problems? Have you and your spouse drifted apart? Are you enduring married life but not enjoying it? If so, you likely feel sad that the warm marital bond you once enjoyed has cooled. As a Christian, you surely would like your marriage to bring glory to Jehovah, the God you love. Hence, your present circumstances may well be a source of concern and heartache to you. Even so, please do not conclude that your situation is hopeless.

² Today, there are fine Christian couples who once had marriages that were merely surviving, not thriving. Yet, they found a way to strengthen their relationship. You too can find more contentment in your marriage. How?

DRAWING CLOSER TO GOD AND TO YOUR SPOUSE

³ You and your spouse will draw closer together if you strive to draw closer to God. Why? Consider an illustration: Imagine a cone-shaped mountain—wide at the base and narrow at the top. A man is standing at the foot of the northern slope while a woman is standing on the other side, at the foot of the southern slope. Both begin

---

1, 2. What question will we consider, and why?
3, 4. Why will marriage mates draw closer together if they strive to draw closer to God? Illustrate.

When applied, Bible knowledge has the power to strengthen your marriage

to climb. When both are still near the mountain base, a long distance separates them. Yet, as each climbs higher and higher toward the narrow summit, the distance between them becomes less and less. Do you see the reassuring lesson in this illustration?

⁴ The effort you put forth to serve Jehovah to the full could be compared with the effort it takes to climb a mountain. Since you love Jehovah, you are already trying hard to climb, so to speak. However, if you and your spouse have grown apart, you may be climbing opposite sides of that mountain. What happens, though, when you continue to climb? Granted, a considerable distance may separate you at first. Nevertheless, the more effort

you put into drawing closer to God—into climbing higher—the closer you and your mate become. Indeed, drawing closer to God is the key to drawing closer to your spouse. But how can you actually do that?

⁵ One important way to climb, as it were, is for you and your spouse to heed the counsel on marriage as found in God's Word. (Psalm 25:4; Isaiah 48:17, 18) Consider, therefore, a specific point of counsel stated by the apostle Paul. He said: "Let marriage be honorable among all." (Hebrews 13:4) What does that mean? The word "honorable" implies that something is esteemed and precious. And that is exactly how Jehovah views marriage—he esteems it as precious.

YOUR MOTIVATION—HEARTFELT LOVE FOR JEHOVAH

⁶ Of course, as servants of God, you and your spouse already *know* that marriage is precious, even sacred. Jehovah himself instituted the marriage arrangement. (Matthew 19:4-6) However, if you are currently experiencing marital problems, just knowing that marriage is honorable may not be enough to motivate you and your mate to treat each other with love and respect. What, then, will move you to do so? Note carefully how Paul addressed the subject of showing honor. He did not say, "marriage *is* honorable"; rather, he said, *"let* marriage *be* honorable." Paul was not merely making an observation; he was giving an exhortation.* Keeping that distinction in

---

* The context shows that Paul's admonition about marriage is part of a series of exhortations.—Hebrews 13:1-5.

---

5. (a) What is one way to draw closer to Jehovah and to one's marriage mate? (b) How does Jehovah view marriage?
6. What does the context of Paul's counsel about marriage show, and why is that important to keep in mind?

mind may help you find added motivation for rekindling esteem for your spouse. Why is that the case?

⁷ Consider for a moment how you regard other Scriptural commands, such as the commission to make disciples or the admonition to meet together for worship. (Matthew 28:19; Hebrews 10:24, 25) Granted, carrying out those commands may at times be a challenge. The people to whom you preach may respond negatively, or the secular work you do may leave you so exhausted that attending Christian meetings is a struggle. Even so, you keep on preaching the Kingdom message, and you keep on attending Christian meetings. No one can stop you—not even Satan! Why not? Because your heartfelt love for Jehovah moves you to obey his commandments. (1 John 5:3) With what good results? Sharing in the preaching work and attending meetings gives you inner peace and heartfelt joy because you know that you are doing God's will. And those feelings, in turn, renew your strength. (Nehemiah 8:10) What is the lesson here?

⁸ Just as your deep love for God moves you to obey the commands to preach and to meet together despite obstacles, so your love for Jehovah can move you to obey the Scriptural exhortation to "let [your] marriage be honorable," even when that appears to be difficult. (Hebrews 13:4; Psalm 18:29; Ecclesiastes 5:4) Additionally, just as your efforts to share in preaching and in meeting together bring rich blessings from God, so your efforts to honor your marriage will be noticed and blessed by Jehovah. —1 Thessalonians 1:3; Hebrews 6:10.

---

7. (a) What Scriptural commands do we carry out, and why? (b) What good results come from obedience?
8, 9. (a) What may move us to obey the exhortation to honor marriage, and why? (b) What two points will we now consider?

⁹ How, then, can you make your marriage honorable? You need to avoid behavior that will damage the marital arrangement. In addition, you need to take steps that will strengthen the marital bond.

AVOID SPEECH AND CONDUCT THAT DISHONOR MARRIAGE

¹⁰ A Christian wife some time ago noted: "I pray to Jehovah for strength to see me through." Through what? She explained: "My husband strikes me with words. I may not have visible bruises, but his constant cutting remarks, such as 'You're a burden!' and 'You're worthless!' have scarred my heart." This wife brings up a matter of grave concern—abusive speech within marriage.

¹¹ How sad it is when spouses in Christian households hurl cruel words at each other, causing emotional wounds that are not easily healed! Obviously, a marriage marked by hurtful speech is not honorable. How is your marriage faring in this regard? One way to find out is by humbly asking your spouse, "What effect do my words have on you?" If your mate feels that time and again your words have caused emotional wounds, you must be willing to change the situation for the better.—Galatians 5: 15; Ephesians 4:31.

¹² Keep clearly in mind that the way in which you use your tongue within the marriage arrangement affects your relationship with Jehovah. The Bible states: "If any man seems to himself to be a formal worshiper and yet does not bridle his tongue, but goes on deceiving his own heart, this man's form of worship is futile." (James 1:26)

10, 11. (a) What conduct dishonors marriage? (b) What question should we consider with our mate?
12. How could one's worship become futile in God's eyes?

Your speech cannot be separated from your worship. The Bible does not support the notion that whatever happens at home is of little consequence as long as one claims to be serving God. Please do not deceive yourself. This is a serious matter. (1 Peter 3:7) You may have abilities and zeal, but if you willfully hurt your spouse with cutting words, you dishonor the marriage arrangement and your worship may be viewed by God as futile.

[13] Marriage partners also need to be alert not to cause emotional pain in less direct ways. Consider two examples: A single mother frequently phones a married Christian man in the congregation to ask him for advice, and they talk at length; a single Christian brother spends considerable time each week working together in the field service with a married Christian sister. The married individuals in those examples may have proper intentions; yet, how does their conduct affect their respective spouses? A wife facing such a situation said: "To note that my husband gives so much time and attention to another sister in the congregation hurts me. It makes me feel inferior."

[14] It is understandable that this spouse and others who face a similar situation in marriage feel hurt. Their mates ignore God's basic instruction for marriage: "A man will leave his father and his mother and he must *stick to his wife*." (Genesis 2:24) Of course, those who marry still respect their parents; however, it is God's arrangement that their foremost obligation is to their spouse. Similarly, Christians dearly love fellow believers; yet their primary responsibility is to their spouse. Thus, when married

---

13. How could a marriage mate cause emotional pain?
14. (a) What marital obligation is highlighted at Genesis 2:24? (b) What should we ask ourselves?

Christians spend inappropriate amounts of time with or become overly familiar with fellow believers, especially those of the opposite sex, they put strains on the marriage bond. Could that be a reason for tension in your marriage? Ask yourself, 'Do I truly give my spouse the time, attention, and affection that rightly belong to my mate?'

¹⁵ Moreover, married Christians who give inappropriate attention to those of the opposite sex who are not their mate unwisely tread on dangerous ground. Sad to say, some married Christians have developed romantic feelings for those with whom they have become overly familiar. (Matthew 5:28) In turn, such emotional bonds have led to conduct that dishonors marriage even more. Consider what the apostle Paul stated about this subject.

"THE MARRIAGE BED BE WITHOUT DEFILEMENT"

¹⁶ Immediately after Paul gave the exhortation to "let marriage be honorable," he added the warning: "[Let] the marriage bed be without defilement, for God will judge fornicators and adulterers." (Hebrews 13:4) Paul used the term "marriage bed" to refer to sexual relations. Such relations are "without defilement," or morally clean, if they are experienced solely within the marriage arrangement. Therefore, Christians heed the inspired words: "Rejoice with the wife of your youth."—Proverbs 5:18.

¹⁷ Those having sexual relations with someone other than their spouse show gross disrespect for God's moral laws. True, many today view adultery as fairly acceptable behavior. Yet, whatever other *humans* may think about adultery should not influence how Christians regard it. They realize that in the end, not man, but *"God* will judge fornicators and adulterers." (Hebrews 10:31; 12:29)

---

15. According to Matthew 5:28, why should married Christians avoid giving inappropriate attention to someone of the opposite sex?
16. What command does Paul give regarding marriage?
17. (a) Why is the world's view of adultery irrelevant to Christians? (b) How can we follow the example set by Job?

Hence, true Christians cling to Jehovah's view on this subject. (Romans 12:9) Recall that the patriarch Job said: "A covenant I have concluded with my eyes." (Job 31:1) Yes, to avoid even one step on the road that could lead to adultery, true Christians control their eyes and never look longingly at a person of the opposite sex who is not their mate.—See the Appendix, pages 219-21.

[18] In Jehovah's eyes, how serious is adultery? The Mosaic Law helps us to appreciate Jehovah's feelings on the matter. In Israel, adultery and idolatry were among the offenses that carried the death penalty. (Leviticus 20:2, 10) Can you see a similarity between the two? Well, an Israelite worshipping an idol broke his covenant with Jehovah. Similarly, an Israelite committing adultery broke his covenant with his spouse. Both acted treacherously. (Exodus 19:5, 6; Deuteronomy 5:9; Malachi 2:14) Hence, both were reprehensible before Jehovah, the faithful and trustworthy God.—Psalm 33:4.

[19] Of course, Christians are not under the Mosaic Law. Yet, recalling that in ancient Israel adultery was viewed in a serious light may strengthen Christians in their resolve not to commit such an act. Why? Consider this comparison: Would you ever enter a church, get down on your knees, and pray in front of an image? 'Never!' you will say. But would you be tempted to do so if you were offered a large sum of money? 'Unthinkable!' you will reply. Indeed, the very thought of betraying Jehovah by worshipping an idol is repulsive to a true Christian. In a similar way, Christians should be repulsed by the thought of betraying their God, Jehovah, as well as

---

18. (a) In Jehovah's eyes, how serious is adultery? (b) What similarity is there between adultery and idolatry?
19. What may strengthen one's resolve to reject adultery, and why?

their spouse by committing adultery—no matter what the incentive to sin might be. (Psalm 51:1, 4; Colossians 3:5) Never do we want to commit an act that would cause Satan to rejoice but would bring grave dishonor to Jehovah and to the sacred marriage arrangement.

HOW TO STRENGTHEN YOUR MARRIAGE BOND

[20] Besides avoiding conduct that dishonors marriage, what steps can you take to rekindle your respect for your marriage mate? To answer, think of the marriage arrangement as being a house. Next, think of the kind words, thoughtful deeds, and other expressions of honor that marriage partners extend to each other as the decorative items that add beauty to a house. If you feel close to each other, your marriage resembles a house adorned with decorations that give it color and warmth. If your affection diminishes, those decorations gradually disappear, leaving your marriage as bleak as a house without any decorations. Since you desire to obey God's command to "let marriage be honorable," you would be moved to improve the situation. After all, something precious and honorable is worth repairing, or restoring. How can you do so? God's Word states: "By wisdom a household will be built up, and by discernment it will prove firmly established. And by knowledge will the interior rooms be filled with all precious and pleasant things of value." (Proverbs 24:3, 4) Consider how these words can be applied to marriage.

[21] Among the 'precious things' filling a happy household are such qualities as true love, godly fear, and

---

20. What has happened in some marriages? Illustrate.
21. How can we gradually strengthen our marriage? (See also the box on page 131.)

HOW CAN I IMPROVE MY MARRIAGE?

Principle: "Let each one of you individually so love his wife as he does himself; on the other hand, the wife should have deep respect for her husband."—Ephesians 5:33.

Some questions to ask yourself

- What are my mate's good qualities, and how can I express appreciation for him or her?—Proverbs 14:1; 31:29; 1 Peter 3:1, 6; 4:8.

- Do I honor my spouse by seeking to understand his or her thoughts and feelings?—Philippians 2:4.

- Am I willing to overlook my spouse's shortcomings?—Matthew 6:14, 15.

- When was the last time I expressed my affection for my spouse?—Song of Solomon 2:9-14.

- Toward what spiritual goals are we working?—Matthew 6:33, 34; 1 Corinthians 9:24-27.

- What initiative can I take to encourage my mate to read the Bible and consider the daily text together with me?

firm faith. (Proverbs 15:16, 17; 1 Peter 1:7) They create a strong marriage. But did you note *how* the rooms in the above-quoted proverb are filled with precious things? "By knowledge." Yes, when applied, Bible knowledge has the power to transform people's thinking and to move them to rekindle their love for each other. (Romans 12:2; Philippians 1:9) Hence, whenever you and your spouse sit down together and calmly consider a Bible passage, such as the daily text, or a Bible-based article in *The Watchtower* or *Awake!* pertaining to marriage, it is as if you were examining a lovely decoration that can beautify your house. When love for Jehovah moves you to apply in your marriage the counsel that you just examined, you are, as it were, bringing that decoration into "the interior rooms." As a result, some of the color and warmth that you once enjoyed in your marriage may return.

²² Granted, it may take considerable time and effort to put those decorations back in place one by one. Yet, if you strive to do your share, you will have the deep satisfaction of knowing that you are obeying the Bible's command: "In showing honor to one another take the lead." (Romans 12:10; Psalm 147:11) Above all, your earnest efforts to honor your marriage will keep you in God's love.

---

22. What satisfaction can we have if we strive to do our share in strengthening our marriage?

Chapter 12

Speak What "Is Good for Building Up"

"Let a rotten saying not proceed out of your mouth,
but whatever saying is good for building up."
—EPHESIANS 4:29.

IF YOU were to give a loved one a gift, how would you feel if he deliberately misused it? Say that you gave him a car, and you later learned that he drove it recklessly, causing injury to others. Would you not be disappointed?

² The ability to utter intelligible speech is a gift from Jehovah, the Giver of "every good gift and every perfect present." (James 1:17) This gift, which sets the human family apart from the animal creation, enables us to convey not just our thoughts but also our feelings to others. Like a motor vehicle, however, the gift of speech can be misused. How it must disappoint Jehovah when speech is used recklessly, causing heartache and pain to others!

³ To remain in God's love, we need to use the gift of speech as the Giver intended. Jehovah leaves no doubt about the kind of speech that pleases him. His Word says: "Let a rotten saying not proceed out of your mouth, but whatever saying is good for building up as the need may be, that it may impart what is favorable to the hearers." (Ephesians 4:29) Let us discuss why we

---

1-3. (a) What is one gift that Jehovah has given us, and how can it be misused? (b) To remain in God's love, how do we need to use the gift of speech?

Calm speech is refreshing

need to keep on guard when it comes to speech, what speech we should avoid, and how we can utter speech that "is good for building up."

WHY WE NEED TO GUARD OUR SPEECH

⁴ One important reason to guard our speech is that *words have power.* Proverbs 15:4 says: "The calmness of the tongue is a tree of life, but distortion in it means a breaking down in the spirit."* Even as water revives a thirsty tree, so the calm speech of a soothing tongue can refresh the spirit of those hearing it. In contrast, the twisted words of a perverse tongue can crush the spirit of others. Indeed, the words we speak have the power to injure or to heal.—Proverbs 18:21.

⁵ Vividly describing the power of words, another proverb says: "There exists the one speaking thoughtlessly as with the stabs of a sword." (Proverbs 12:18) Thoughtless words said in haste can cause deep emotional wounds and destroy relationships. Has your heart ever been pierced by the thrusts of a verbal sword? On the positive side, the same proverb says: "The tongue of the

---

* The Hebrew word rendered "distortion" at Proverbs 15:4 can also mean "crookedness, perverseness."

4, 5. How do some Bible proverbs describe the power of words?

wise ones is a healing." Thoughtful words from one who manifests godly wisdom can mend an aching heart and restore relationships. Can you recall an occasion when you experienced the healing power of kind words? (Proverbs 16:24) Recognizing that spoken words have power, we certainly want to use our speech to heal others, not to hurt them.

⁶ No matter how hard we try, we cannot completely control our tongue. Here, then, is a second reason why we need to keep on guard respecting our speech: *Sin and imperfection incline us toward misusing our tongue.* Words are a product of our heart, and "the inclination of the heart of man is bad." (Genesis 8:21; Luke 6:45) Bridling our tongue is therefore a real struggle. (James 3: 2-4) Although we cannot gain perfect control of our tongue, we can keep working at making improvement in how we use it. Just as a swimmer trying to swim upstream has to keep fighting the current, so we have to keep fighting the sinful tendency to misuse our tongue.

⁷ A third reason to guard our speech is that *Jehovah holds us accountable for our words.* The way we use our tongue affects not only our relationship with fellow humans but also our standing with Jehovah. James 1:26 says: "If any man seems to himself to be a formal worshiper and yet does not bridle his tongue, but goes on deceiving his own heart, this man's form of worship is futile."* As we saw in the preceding chapter, our speech is not independent of our worship. If our tongue is

---

* The Greek word translated "futile" is also rendered "useless" and "fruitless."—1 Corinthians 15:17; 1 Peter 1:18.

---

6. Why is it a real struggle to control our tongue?
7, 8. To what extent does Jehovah hold us accountable for our words?

unbridled—spewing out hurtful, poisonous speech—all of our Christian works could be rendered worthless in God's eyes. Is that not a sobering thought?—James 3: 8-10.

⁸ It is clear that we have strong reasons to guard against misusing the gift of speech. Before we consider wholesome forms of speech that build up, let us discuss speech that certainly has no place in the life of a true Christian.

SPEECH THAT TEARS DOWN

⁹ *Obscene language.* Cursing, profanity, and other forms of obscene language are part of everyday speech in today's world. Many resort to expletives to emphasize their speech or to compensate for an otherwise limited vocabulary. Comedians often use vulgar, sex-oriented speech to make people laugh. Obscene language, however, is no laughing matter. Some 2,000 years ago, the inspired apostle Paul counseled the Colossian congregation to put away "obscene talk." (Colossians 3:8) Paul told the Ephesian congregation that "obscene jesting" is among things that should "not even be mentioned among" true Christians.—Ephesians 5:3, 4.

¹⁰ Obscene speech is offensive to Jehovah. It is also offensive to those who love him. Indeed, our love for Jehovah moves us to reject obscene language. When listing "the works of the flesh," Paul cites "uncleanness," which can include impurity in speech. (Galatians 5:19-21) This is a serious matter. An individual can be disfellowshipped from the congregation if despite repeat-

---

9, 10. (a) What kind of language has become part of everyday speech in today's world? (b) Why do we need to reject obscene language? (See also footnote.)

ed counsel he unrepentantly makes a practice of using speech that refers to or promotes what is grossly immoral, degrading, and corrupting.*

¹¹ *Harmful gossip, slander.* Gossip is idle talk about people and their lives. Is all gossip bad? Not if we mean innocent conversation in which we might share positive or helpful news, such as who just got baptized or who needs a word of encouragement. First-century Christians had a keen interest in one another's welfare and shared appropriate information about fellow believers. (Ephesians 6:21, 22; Colossians 4:8, 9) Gossip, however, can be harmful if it distorts the facts or reveals private matters. Even more serious, it can lead to slander, which is always damaging. Slander is "the utterance of false charges . . . which defame and damage another's reputation." The Pharisees, for example, resorted to malicious slander in an attempt to discredit Jesus. (Matthew 9:32-34; 12:22-24) Slander often causes contention.—Proverbs 26:20.

¹² Jehovah does not view lightly those who use the gift of speech to defame others or to cause divisions. He hates those causing "contentions among brothers." (Proverbs 6:16-19) The Greek word rendered "slanderer" is *di·a′bo·los,* which is also used as a title of Satan. He is the "Devil," the evil slanderer of God. (Revelation 12: 9, 10) Surely we want to avoid speech that would cause us to become, in effect, a devil. There is no room in the

---

* As used in the Scriptures, "uncleanness" is a broad term that can cover a wide range of sins. Although not all uncleanness warrants judicial action, an individual can be expelled from the congregation if he unrepentantly practices *gross* uncleanness.—2 Corinthians 12:21; Ephesians 4:19; see "Questions From Readers" in *The Watchtower* of July 15, 2006.

11, 12. (a) What is gossip, and how can it become harmful? (b) Why do worshippers of Jehovah need to avoid slanderous speech?

congregation for slanderous speech that stirs up such works of the flesh as "contentions" and "divisions." (Galatians 5:19-21) Hence, before repeating some news about someone, ask yourself: 'Is it true? Would it be kind to repeat this? Is it necessary or advisable to share this information?'—1 Thessalonians 4:11.

[13] *Abusive speech.* As previously noted, words have the power to hurt. Admittedly, at times because of human imperfection, we all say things we regret. However, the Bible warns about a pattern of speech that has absolutely no place in a Christian home or in the congregation. Paul admonished Christians: "Let all malicious bitterness and anger and wrath and screaming and abusive speech be taken away from you." (Ephesians 4:31) Other translations render the phrase "abusive speech" as "evil words," "injurious language," and "insulting language." Abusive speech—including degrading name-calling and harsh, relentless criticism—can strip others of their dignity and leave them feeling worthless. The tender and trusting hearts of children are especially vulnerable to the crushing effects of abusive speech.—Colossians 3:21.

[14] In the strongest possible terms, the Bible condemns reviling—the practice of vilifying others with insulting, derogatory, or abusive language. An individual who makes a practice of such speech puts himself in a dangerous position, for a reviler can be removed from the congregation if he fails to heed repeated efforts to help him change. Unless he changes his ways, he could also lose out on Kingdom blessings. (1 Corinthians 5:11-13; 6:9, 10) Clearly, then, there is no way for us to remain in

---

13, 14. (a) What effect can abusive speech have on its hearers? (b) What is reviling, and why does a reviler put himself in a dangerous position?

God's love if we make a practice of uttering speech that is unwholesome, untrue, or unkind. Such speech tears down.

WORDS THAT ARE "GOOD FOR BUILDING UP"

[15] How can we use the gift of speech as the Giver intended? Recall that God's Word urges us to speak "whatever saying is good for building up." (Ephesians 4:29) Jehovah is pleased when we speak words that build up, encourage, and strengthen others. It takes thought to speak such words. The Bible does not provide a set formula to follow; neither does it contain a list of approved types of "wholesome speech." (Titus 2:8) To utter words that are "good for building up," we do well to keep in mind three simple but important factors that characterize upbuilding speech: It is wholesome, it is true, and it is kind. With such factors in mind, let us consider a few specific examples of speech that builds up.—See the box "Is My Speech Upbuilding?" on page 140.

[16] *Sincere commendation.* Both Jehovah and Jesus recognize the need to speak words of commendation and approval. (Matthew 3:17; 25:19-23; John 1:47) As Christians, we too do well to offer genuine commendation to others. Why? "A word at its right time is O how good!" says Proverbs 15:23. Just ask yourself: 'How do I feel when I receive heartfelt commendation? Does it not warm my heart and lift my spirits?' Indeed, a sincere word of commendation lets you know that someone notices you, that someone cares about you, and that what you did was well worth the effort involved. Such

---

15. What kind of speech "is good for building up"?
16, 17. (a) Why should we commend others? (b) What opportunities are there to commend others in the congregation? in the family?

IS MY SPEECH UPBUILDING?

Principle: "Let your utterance be always with graciousness."—Colossians 4:6.

Some questions to ask yourself

■ When was the last time I offered someone specific commendation?—1 Corinthians 11:2; Revelation 2:1-3.

■ Do I express my respect for others by saying please and thank you?—Genesis 13:14; John 11:41.

■ In conversation, do I speak mainly about myself, or am I also interested in the thoughts and feelings of others?—Philippians 2:3, 4; James 1:19.

■ Do I use what I know about others as a means to build them up or to tear them down?—Proverbs 15:1, 2.

■ How do I feel about the use of profanity, and what does my view reveal about what is in my heart?—Luke 6:45; James 3:10, 11.

Speak What "Is Good for Building Up"

reassurance builds your confidence and motivates you to work even more diligently in the future. Since you appreciate it when you *receive* commendation, should you not, in turn, do your best to *give* commendation to others?—Matthew 7:12.

[17] Train yourself to look for the good in others, and then give voice to the positive. In the congregation, you may hear a well-developed talk at a meeting, notice a young one who is reaching out for spiritual goals, or observe an older one who is faithful in attending meetings despite the limitations of advancing years. A sincere word of commendation may touch the hearts of such ones and strengthen them spiritually. In the family, husbands and wives need to hear words of warm commendation and appreciation from each other. (Proverbs 31: 10, 28) Especially do children thrive on feeling noticed and appreciated. Commendation and approval are to a child what sunshine and water are to a plant. Parents, look for opportunities to commend your children for their praiseworthy qualities and efforts. Such commendation can build courage and confidence in your children and motivate them to try even harder to do what is right.

[18] *Comfort and consolation.* Jehovah deeply cares about "the lowly ones" and "the ones being crushed." (Isaiah 57:15) His Word urges us to "keep comforting one another" and to "speak consolingly to the depressed souls." (1 Thessalonians 5:11, 14) We can be sure that God notices and appreciates our efforts to comfort and console fellow believers whose hearts are weighed down with sadness.

18, 19. Why should we do our best to comfort and console fellow believers, and how can we do so?

¹⁹ What, though, can you say to build up a fellow Christian who is discouraged or depressed? Do not feel that you must fix the problem. In many cases, simple words are often the most helpful. Assure the downhearted person of your care and concern. Offer to pray aloud with the discouraged one; you can beseech Jehovah to help that one to know how much he or she is loved by others and by God. (James 5:14, 15) Reassure him that he is needed and valued as a member of the congregation. (1 Corinthians 12:12-26) Read an encouraging Bible verse to assure him that Jehovah truly cares about him as an individual. (Psalm 34:18; Matthew 10:29-31) Taking ample time to share a "good word" with the despondent one and speaking from your heart will no doubt help him to feel loved and appreciated. —Proverbs 12:25.

Jehovah is pleased when we speak words that build others up

²⁰ *Effective counsel.* As imperfect creatures, we all need to receive counsel from time to time. The Bible encourages us: "Listen to counsel and accept discipline, in order that you may become wise in your future." (Proverbs 19:20) Giving counsel to others is not limited to the elders. Parents counsel children. (Ephesians 6:4) Mature sisters

---

20, 21. What factors make counsel effective?

Speak What "Is Good for Building Up"

may need to offer counsel to younger women. (Titus 2:3-5) Love for others moves us to want to give counsel that the recipient can accept without feeling crushed. What can help us to give such counsel? Consider three factors that make counsel more effective: the attitude and motive of the counselor, the basis for the counsel, and the manner in which it is given.

21 Effective counsel starts with the counselor. Ask yourself, 'When is counsel easy for me to accept?' When you know that the one counseling you cares about you, is not speaking out of personal frustration, and has no ulterior motives, the counsel is easier to accept. So when you counsel others, should not the same things be true of your attitude and motive? Successful counsel is also based on God's Word. (2 Timothy 3:16) Whether directly quoting from the Bible or not, we should have a Scriptural basis for any counsel we give. Thus, elders are careful not to impose their own views on others; neither do they bend or twist the Scriptures, making it seem that the Bible supports some personal view. Counsel is also more effective if it is delivered in the right manner. Counsel that is salted with kindness is easier to accept and lets the one receiving it keep his dignity.—Colossians 4:6.

22 To be sure, speech is a precious gift from God. Our love for Jehovah should move us to use, not misuse, this gift. Let us remember that the words we speak to others have power—the power to build up or to tear down. Let us, then, strive to use this gift as the Giver intended —"for building up." Our speech will thus be a blessing to those around us and will help us to remain in God's love.

---

22. What is your determination regarding the use of the gift of speech?

CHAPTER 13

Celebrations That Displease God

"Keep on making sure of what is acceptable to the Lord."—EPHESIANS 5:10.

"THE true worshipers," said Jesus, "will worship the Father with spirit and truth, for, indeed, the Father is looking for suchlike ones to worship him." (John 4:23) When Jehovah finds such individuals—as he found you—he draws them to himself and to his Son. (John 6:44) What an honor that is! Lovers of Bible truth, however, must "keep on making sure of what is acceptable to the Lord," for Satan is a master of deception.—Ephesians 5:10; Revelation 12:9.

² Consider what occurred near Mount Sinai when the Israelites asked Aaron to make them a god. Aaron acquiesced and made a golden calf but implied that it represented Jehovah. "There is a festival to Jehovah tomorrow," he said. Was Jehovah indifferent to this fusion of true religion and false? No. He had about three thousand idolaters put to death. (Exodus 32:1-6, 10, 28) The lesson? If we want to keep ourselves in God's love, we must "touch nothing unclean" and jealously guard the truth against any form of corruption.—Isaiah 52:11; Ezekiel 44: 23; Galatians 5:9.

---

1. What kind of people does Jehovah draw to himself, and why must they remain spiritually vigilant?
2. Explain how Jehovah views those who try to fuse true religion with false.

Celebrations That Displease God

³ Sadly, after the death of the apostles, who acted as a restraint against apostasy, so-called Christians who had no love of truth began to adopt pagan customs, celebrations, and "holy" days, which they dubbed Christian. (2 Thessalonians 2:7, 10) As you consider some of these celebrations, note how they reflect, not the spirit of God, but that of the world. Generally speaking, worldly celebrations have a common theme: They appeal to fleshly desires, and they promote false religious beliefs and spiritism—the hallmarks of "Babylon the Great."* (Revelation 18:2-4, 23) Keep in mind, too, that Jehovah observed firsthand the disgusting pagan religious practices from which many popular customs originated. No doubt he finds such celebrations just as offensive today. Should not his view be what matters most to us?—2 John 6, 7.

⁴ As true Christians, we know that certain celebrations are not pleasing to Jehovah. But we need to be firmly determined in our heart to have absolutely nothing to do with them. A review of why Jehovah is displeased with such celebrations will strengthen our resolve to avoid anything that might hinder us from remaining in God's love.

CHRISTMAS—SUN WORSHIP RENAMED

⁵ The Bible makes no mention of a birthday celebration for Jesus. In fact, his exact birth date is unknown. We can be sure, though, that he was not born on December 25 in the cold of winter in that part of the

---

* See the box "Should I Join in the Celebration?" on pages 148-9. A number of specific "holy" days and celebrations are listed in the *Watch Tower Publications Index*, published by Jehovah's Witnesses.

3, 4. Why should we pay close attention to Bible principles when examining popular customs and celebrations?
5. Why can we be certain that Jesus was not born on December 25?

world.* For one thing, Luke recorded that when Jesus was born, "shepherds [were] living out of doors" minding their flocks. (Luke 2:8-11) If "living out of doors" had been their habit year round, that would not have been noteworthy. However, because Bethlehem is subject to cold rains and snow, flocks were wintered under cover and shepherds would not have been "living out of doors." Additionally, Joseph and Mary went to Bethlehem because Caesar Augustus had ordered a census. (Luke 2:1-7) It is highly unlikely that Caesar would have commanded a people who were resentful of Roman rule to travel to their ancestral cities in the dead of winter.

⁶ The roots of Christmas are found, not in Scripture, but in ancient pagan festivals, such as the Roman Saturnalia, a celebration dedicated to Saturn, the god of agriculture. Likewise, according to their reckoning, devotees of the god Mithra celebrated December 25 as the "birthday of the invincible sun," says the *New Catholic Encyclopedia.* "Christmas originated at a time when the cult of the sun was particularly strong at Rome," about three centuries after the death of Christ.

⁷ During their celebrations, pagans exchanged gifts and feasted—practices that Christmas preserved. As is also true today, however, much Christmas giving was not in the spirit of 2 Corinthians 9:7, which reads: "Let each one do just as he has resolved in his heart, not grudgingly or under compulsion, for God loves a cheerful giver." True

---

* Based on Biblical reckoning and secular history, Jesus was likely born in 2 B.C.E. in the Jewish month of Ethanim, which corresponds to September/October on our present calendar.—See *Insight on the Scriptures,* Volume 2, pages 56-7, published by Jehovah's Witnesses.

6, 7. (a) The roots of many Christmas customs can be found where? (b) What contrast can be seen between Christmas giving and Christian giving?

True Christians give out of love

Christians give out of love, their giving is not tied to a date, and they expect no gifts in return. (Luke 14:12-14; Acts 20:35) Moreover, they deeply appreciate being set free from the Christmas frenzy and relieved of the heavy yoke of financial debt that many incur at that time of year.—Matthew 11:28-30; John 8:32.

⁸ But, some may argue, did not the astrologers present birthday gifts to Jesus? No. Their gift-giving was simply a way of paying their respects to a person of note, a common custom in Bible times. (1 Kings 10:1, 2, 10, 13; Matthew 2:2, 11) In fact, they did not even come on the night that Jesus was born. Jesus was, not a babe in a manger, but many months old and living in a house when they arrived.

---

8. Did the astrologers present birthday gifts to Jesus? Explain.

SHOULD I JOIN IN THE CELEBRATION?

Principle: " 'Get out from among them, and separate yourselves,' says Jehovah, 'and quit touching the unclean thing'; 'and I will take you in.' "—2 Corinthians 6:17.

Some questions to ask yourself about a popular celebration or custom

- Does it clearly have roots in a false religious practice or teaching, including spiritism?—Isaiah 52:11; 1 Corinthians 4:6; 2 Corinthians 6:14-18; Revelation 18:4.

- Does it give undue honor or adulation to a human, an organization, or a national symbol?—Jeremiah 17:5-7; Acts 10:25, 26; 1 John 5:21.

- Does it elevate one nation or ethnic group over another?—Acts 10:34, 35; 17:26.

- Does it reflect "the spirit of the world," which works in opposition to God's holy spirit?—1 Corinthians 2:12; Ephesians 2:2.

- Could my participation in it be a cause for stumbling?—Romans 14:21.

- If I choose not to participate, how would I respectfully explain my reasons to others?—Romans 12:1, 2; Colossians 4:6.

The following scriptures may shed further light on questions about popular observances:

- "[Unfaithful Israelites] went mingling with the nations and took up learning their works."—Psalm 106:35.

- "The person faithful in what is least is faithful also in much, and the person unrighteous in what is least is unrighteous also in much." —Luke 16:10.
- "You are no part of the world." —John 15:19.
- "You cannot be partaking of 'the table of Jehovah' and the table of demons." —1 Corinthians 10:21.
- "The time that has passed by is sufficient for you to have worked out the will of the nations when you proceeded in deeds of loose conduct, lusts, excesses with wine, revelries, drinking matches, and illegal idolatries." —1 Peter 4:3.

BIBLICAL LIGHT ON BIRTHDAYS

⁹ Even though the birth of a baby has always been a cause for much joy, the Bible makes no reference to a birthday celebration for a servant of God. (Psalm 127:3) Was this simply an oversight? No, for two birthday celebrations are mentioned—that of a Pharaoh of Egypt and that of Herod Antipas. (Genesis 40:20-22; Mark 6:21-29) Both events, however, are presented in a bad light—especially the latter, which saw John the Baptizer beheaded.

¹⁰ "The early Christians," notes *The World Book Ency-*

---

9. What is significant about birthday celebrations mentioned in the Bible?
10, 11. How did the early Christians view birthday celebrations, and why?

"HOLY" DAYS AND SATANISM

It is of interest to note that the most important day in the religion called Satanism is one's birthday. Why? Because Satanists hold that each individual is a god if he chooses to view himself as one. Thus, to celebrate one's own birthday is to celebrate the birth of a god. Of course, most people do not take such an extreme, egotistical view. Nevertheless, the book *The Lore of Birthdays* states: "Other holidays lift the heart, but birthdays warm the ego."

The next most "holy" days on the Satanists' calendar are Walpurgis Night and Halloween. *Merriam-Webster's Collegiate Dictionary* defines the former as "the eve of May Day on which witches are held to ride to an appointed rendezvous."

clopedia, "considered the celebration of anyone's birth to be a pagan custom." The ancient Greeks, for instance, believed that each person had a protective spirit that attended the person's birth and thereafter watched over him. That spirit "had a mystic relation with the god on whose birthday the individual was born," says the book *The Lore of Birthdays.* Birthdays also have a long-standing and an intimate link with astrology and the horoscope.

¹¹ Besides rejecting birthday customs on account of pagan and spiritistic roots, God's servants of old likely rejected them on principle as well. Why? These were humble, modest men and women who did not view their arrival in the world as so important that it should be celebrated.* (Micah 6:8; Luke 9:48) Rather, they glorified Jehovah and thanked him for the precious gift of life.#
—Psalm 8:3, 4; 36:9; Revelation 4:11.

¹² At death, all integrity-keepers are safe in God's memory, and their future life is guaranteed. (Job 14:14, 15) Says Ecclesiastes 7:1: "A name is better than good oil, and the day of death than the day of one's being born." Our "name" is the good reputation we have gained with God through faithful service. Significantly, the only commemoration commanded for Christians involves, not a birth, but a death—that of Jesus, whose excellent "name" is the key to our salvation.—Luke 22:17-20; Hebrews 1:3, 4.

---

* See the box " 'Holy' Days and Satanism," on page 150.

The Law covenant required that a woman, after giving birth, present a sin offering to God. (Leviticus 12:1-8) A poignant reminder that humans pass sin on to their children, this legal requirement helped the Israelites to have a balanced view of the birth of a child and may have discouraged them from adopting pagan birthday customs.—Psalm 51:5.

12. How can the day of our death be better than the day of our birth?

EASTER—FERTILITY WORSHIP IN DISGUISE

¹³ Promoted as a celebration of Christ's resurrection, Easter is actually rooted in false religion. The name Easter itself has been linked to Eostre, or Ostara, the Anglo-Saxon goddess of the dawn and of spring. And how did eggs and rabbits come to be associated with Easter? Eggs "have been prominent as symbols of new life and resurrection," says the *Encyclopædia Britannica,* while the hare and the rabbit have long served as symbols of fertility. Easter, therefore, is really a fertility rite thinly disguised as a celebration of Christ's resurrection.*

¹⁴ Would Jehovah condone the use of a filthy fertility rite to commemorate his Son's resurrection? Never! (2 Corinthians 6:17, 18) In fact, the Scriptures neither command nor authorize the commemorating of Jesus' resurrection in the first place. To do so in the name of Easter, therefore, is to be doubly disloyal.

HALLOWEEN IS FAR FROM HOLY

¹⁵ Known for its witches, goblins, and other grotesque decorations and paraphernalia, Halloween—also called All Hallows' Eve or the eve of All Saints' Day—can be traced back to the ancient Celts of Britain and Ireland. On the full moon nearest November 1, they celebrated the festival of Samhain, meaning "Summer's End." They

---

* Easter has also been linked to the worship of the Phoenician fertility goddess, Astarte, who had as her symbols the egg and the hare. Statues of Astarte have variously depicted her as having exaggerated sex organs or with a rabbit beside her and an egg in her hand.

13, 14. What are the roots of popular Easter customs?
15. What is the origin of Halloween, and what may be significant about the date chosen to celebrate this holiday?

believed that during Samhain, the veil between the human and the supernatural worlds was parted and that spirits, both good and evil, roamed the earth. The souls of the dead were thought to return to their homes, and families would put out food and drink for their ghostly visitors in hopes of appeasing them. Thus, when children today, dressed as ghosts or witches, go from house to house threatening a mischievous trick unless they receive a treat, they unwittingly perpetuate the rituals of Samhain.

KEEP YOUR WEDDING UNDEFILED

[16] Soon, "no voice of a bridegroom and of a bride will ever be heard in [Babylon the Great] again." (Revelation 18:23) Why? In part because of her spiritistic practices, which can defile a marriage right from the wedding day. —Mark 10:6-9.

[17] Customs vary from country to country. Some customs that may appear innocent may have their roots in Babylonish practices that are supposed to bring 'good luck' to the bridal couple or their guests. (Isaiah 65:11) One such tradition involves the throwing of rice or its substitutes. This practice may have had its roots in the notion that food appeased evil spirits and kept them from doing injury to the bride and groom. Additionally, rice has a long mystical association with fertility, happiness, and longevity. Clearly, all who want to remain in God's love will shun such tainted customs.—2 Corinthians 6:14-18.

16, 17. (a) Why should Christian couples planning to get married examine local wedding customs in the light of Bible principles? (b) In regard to such customs as throwing rice or its substitutes, what should Christians take into consideration?

¹⁸ Servants of Jehovah likewise refrain from worldly practices that may rob weddings and wedding receptions of Christian dignity or that may offend the conscience of some. For example, they avoid giving speeches tainted with hurtful sarcasm or sexual innuendos and refrain from practical jokes or remarks that can embarrass the newlyweds and others. (Proverbs 26:18, 19; Luke 6:31; 10: 27) They also avoid lavish fairy-tale receptions that reflect, not modesty, but "the showy display of one's means of life." (1 John 2:16) If you are planning a wedding, never forget that Jehovah wants your special day to be something you can always look back on with joy, not regret.*

TOASTING—A RELIGIOUS GESTURE?

¹⁹ A common practice at weddings and on other social occasions is toasting. The 1995 *International Handbook on Alcohol and Culture* says: "Toasting . . . is probably a secular vestige of ancient sacrificial libations in which a sacred liquid was offered to the gods . . . in exchange for a wish, a prayer summarized in the words 'long life!' or 'to your health!' "

²⁰ True, many people may not consciously view toasting as a religious or superstitious gesture. Still, the custom of lifting wine glasses heavenward might be viewed as a request to "heaven"—a superhuman force—for a blessing in a way that does not accord with that outlined in the Scriptures.—John 14:6; 16:23.#

---

* See the three articles on weddings and social gatherings in *The Watchtower*, October 15, 2006, pages 18-31.
\# See *The Watchtower*, February 15, 2007, pages 30-1.

---

18. What Bible principles should guide both the couple planning a wedding and those invited to attend?
19, 20. What does one secular source say about the origin of toasting, and why is this custom unacceptable to Christians?

"YOU LOVERS OF JEHOVAH, HATE WHAT IS BAD"

21 Reflecting the plummeting standards of today's world—a trend promoted either directly or indirectly by Babylon the Great—some countries sponsor annual carnivals or Mardi Gras, festivals that feature lewd dancing and that may even celebrate gay and lesbian lifestyles. Would it be appropriate for a 'lover of Jehovah' to attend or view such an event? Would his doing so reflect a genuine hatred for what is bad? (Psalm 1:1, 2; 97:10) How much better to imitate the attitude of the psalmist who prayed: "Make my eyes pass on from seeing what is worthless"!—Psalm 119:37.

22 On the days of worldly celebrations, a Christian would be careful that his conduct not give others the impression that he is joining in the celebration. "Whether you are eating or drinking or doing anything else," wrote Paul, "do all things for God's glory." (1 Corinthians 10:31; see the box "Making Wise Decisions," on pages 158-9.) On the other hand, if a custom or a celebration clearly retains no false religious significance, is not part of a political or patriotic observance, and violates no Bible principles, then each Christian might make a personal decision as to whether he will share in it. At the same time, he would consider the feelings of others so as not to become a cause for stumbling.

GLORIFY GOD IN WORD AND DEED

23 Many people view the days of certain popular celebrations primarily as opportunities for family and

---

21. Even though they may not have a religious theme, what popular celebrations would Christians avoid, and why?
22. When might a Christian decide according to his own conscience whether he will share in a celebration or not?
23, 24. How might we give a good witness concerning Jehovah's righteous standards?

TRUE WORSHIP BRINGS THE GREATEST JOY

Jehovah is "the happy God," and he wants his servants to be happy. (1 Timothy 1:11) This fact is reflected in the following scriptures:

"The one that is good at heart has a feast constantly."—Proverbs 15:15.

"I have come to know that there is nothing better for them than to rejoice and to do good during one's life; and also that every man should eat and indeed drink and see good for all his hard work. It is the gift of God."—Ecclesiastes 3:12, 13.

"As regards the generous one, it is for generous things that he has given counsel; and in favor of generous things he himself will rise up."—Isaiah 32:8.

"Come to me, all you who are toiling and loaded down, and I [Jesus] will refresh you. . . . For my yoke is kindly and my load is light."—Matthew 11:28, 30.

"You will know the truth, and the truth will set you free."—John 8:32.

"Let each one [give] just as he has resolved in his heart, not grudgingly or under compulsion, for God loves a cheerful giver."—2 Corinthians 9:7.

"The fruitage of the spirit is love, joy, peace, . . . kindness, goodness."—Galatians 5:22.

"The fruitage of the light consists of every sort of goodness and righteousness and truth."—Ephesians 5:9.

friends to get together. Thus, if someone wrongly assumes that our Scriptural stand is unloving or extreme, we can kindly explain that Jehovah's Witnesses value wholesome gatherings of family and friends. (Proverbs 11:25; Ecclesiastes 3:12, 13; 2 Corinthians 9:7) We enjoy fellowship with loved ones throughout the year, but because of our love for God and for his righteous standards, we do not want to tarnish such happy occasions with customs that offend him.—See the box "True Worship Brings the Greatest Joy," on page 156.

24 Some Witnesses have had good success in sharing with sincere inquirers points from chapter 16 of the book *What Does the Bible Really Teach?** Remember, though, that our goal is to win hearts, not arguments. So be respectful, maintain a mild temper, and "let your utterance be always with graciousness, seasoned with salt."—Colossians 4:6.

25 As Jehovah's servants, we are well-informed. We know why we believe and practice certain things and abstain from others. (Hebrews 5:14) So parents, teach your children to reason on Bible principles. By doing so, you build up their faith, you help them to give Scriptural answers to those who question their beliefs, and you assure them of Jehovah's love.—Isaiah 48:17, 18; 1 Peter 3:15.

26 All who worship God "with spirit and truth" not only avoid unscriptural celebrations but also strive to be honest in every aspect of life. Today, many view honesty as impractical. But as we shall see in the next chapter, God's ways are always the best.

---

* Published by Jehovah's Witnesses.

25, 26. How can parents help their children to grow in faith and love for Jehovah?

MAKING WISE DECISIONS

At times, situations may arise that test our love for Jehovah and our grasp of Bible principles. For example, a Christian's unbelieving marriage mate may invite him or her to have a meal with relatives on a worldly holiday. Some Christians may in good conscience accept; others may not. If a Christian does accept such an offer, his conduct should make it plain that he is not celebrating the holiday and that his visit is purely to enjoy a meal with relatives.

It would be prudent for a Christian to speak respectfully to his marriage mate in advance, explaining the embarrassment that might occur if the relatives share in holiday activities and the Witness declines. The unbelieving mate might decide to visit on another day.—1 Peter 3:15.

After hearing his wife's explanation, what if the husband of a Christian woman still insists that she accompany him? She might conclude that as head of the household, he has the responsibility to provide food for the family. (Colossians 3:18) In this case, the meal is at the home of his relatives. She may even be able to give a fine witness on that occasion. The food is not contaminated just because it is eaten on a worldly holiday. (1 Corinthians 8:8) The Christian might view it as a common meal and not join in any holiday greetings, songs, toasts, and so forth.

Another factor to be considered is the effect that sharing in such a meal might have on others. A Christian wife should take into account the possibility that others who learn of her visit with worldly relatives on that day might be stumbled.—1 Corinthians 8:9; 10:23, 24.

In addition, will the family pressure the Christian wife to compromise? The desire to avoid any embarrassment can exert a powerful influence! So it would be important to think the matter through in advance, taking all these factors into consideration, including, of course, her own Christian conscience.—Acts 24:16.

Should I Accept a Christmas Bonus?

During the Christmas season, a Christian's employer may offer a present or a bonus. Should the Christian reject such? Not necessarily. The employer may not even be thinking that by accepting the bonus the receiver is celebrating Christmas. The employer may simply be giving all his workers a share of the company's profits. Or the bonus may be evidence of his gratitude for services rendered all year long as well as a stimulus to continued good work. The employer may give a gift to all employees—Jews, Muslims, or others—regardless of whether they celebrate Christmas or not. So the mere timing of the gift or the name that may be associated with it does not necessarily rule out its acceptance by one of Jehovah's Witnesses.

Even if the gift is given because of a religious holiday, that does not mean that the recipient is thought to share the religious view. A fellow worker or a relative may tell a Witness, "I know that you do not celebrate this holiday, but I still want you to have this as a gift from me." If the Christian's conscience would be at rest, he might choose to accept the gift and express thanks without any reference to the holiday. (Acts 23:1) Perhaps at a time when there will be less likelihood of causing offense, the Christian can tactfully explain his stand.

However, what if the one offering the gift has the clear intention of showing that the Christian is not firm in his beliefs or will compromise for material gain? Then it is definitely best to decline. To be sure, we want to render Jehovah God exclusive devotion.—Matthew 4:8-10.

CHAPTER 14

Be Honest in All Things

"We wish to conduct ourselves honestly in all things."—HEBREWS 13:18.

A MOTHER and her little boy leave a store together. Suddenly, the child stops, a look of shock on his face. In his hand he is holding a small toy that he picked up in the store. He forgot to put it back or to ask his mother if she would buy it. He cries out to her, distressed. She reassures him and takes him back into the store so that he can return the item and apologize. As he does so, the mother's heart swells with joy and pride. Why?

² Few things delight parents more than seeing that their children are learning the importance of honesty. And so it is with our heavenly Father, "the God of truth." (Psalm 31:5) As he watches us grow to spiritual maturity, he is pleased to see us striving to be honest. Because we want to please him and remain in his love, we echo the sentiments expressed by the apostle Paul: "We wish to conduct ourselves honestly in all things." (Hebrews 13:18) Let us focus on four main areas of life in which we may at times find it a special challenge to be honest. Then we will consider some of the blessings that come as a result.

HONESTY WITH OURSELVES

³ Our first challenge is to learn to be honest with our-

1, 2. Why is Jehovah pleased when he sees our efforts to be honest? Illustrate.
3-5. (a) How does God's Word warn us about the dangers of self-deception? (b) What will help us to be honest with ourselves?

selves. It is very easy for us as imperfect humans to succumb to self-deception. For instance, Jesus told the Christians in Laodicea that they had fooled themselves into thinking that they were rich when, in fact, they were "poor and blind and naked" spiritually—a truly pitiable state. (Revelation 3:17) Their self-deception only made their situation more dangerous.

⁴ You may recall, too, that the disciple James warned: "If any man seems to himself to be a formal worshiper and yet does not bridle his tongue, but goes on deceiving his own heart, this man's form of worship is futile." (James 1:26) If we were to reason that we could misuse our tongue and still worship Jehovah acceptably, we would succeed only in deceiving our own heart. Our worship of Jehovah would be futile, an utter waste. What can keep us from such a sad course?

⁵ In that same passage, James likens the truth of God's word to a mirror. He advises us to peer into God's perfect law and make adjustments accordingly. (James 1:23-25) The Bible can help us to be honest with ourselves and to see what we need to do to improve. (Lamentations 3:40; Haggai 1:5) We may also pray to Jehovah and ask him to examine us, helping us to see and to address any serious flaws. (Psalm 139:23, 24) Dishonesty is an insidious weakness, and we need to view it as our heavenly Father does. Proverbs 3:32 says: "The devious person is a detestable thing to Jehovah, but His intimacy is with the upright ones." Jehovah can help us to feel as he does and to see ourselves as he sees us. Remember that Paul said: "We *wish* to conduct ourselves honestly." We cannot be perfect now, but we sincerely desire and earnestly seek to be honest.

HONESTY IN THE FAMILY

⁶ Honesty should be a hallmark of the Christian family. Husband and wife, then, must be open and honest with each other. There is no room in a Christian marriage for such hurtful, unclean practices as flirting with those outside the marriage, cultivating clandestine relationships via the Internet, or using pornography in any form. Some married Christians have taken up such wrong conduct while concealing it from an innocent mate. Doing so is dishonest. Notice the words of faithful King David: "I have not sat with men of untruth; and with those who hide what they are I do not come in." (Psalm 26:4) If you are married, never engage in conduct that might tempt you to hide what you are from your mate!

⁷ In teaching their children the value of honesty, parents are wise to make use of Bible examples. On the negative side, there are such accounts as that of Achan, who stole and attempted to cover his theft; Gehazi, who lied for the sake of financial gain; and Judas, who stole and lied spitefully to harm Jesus.—Joshua 6:17-19; 7:11-25; 2 Kings 5:14-16, 20-27; Matthew 26:14, 15; John 12:6.

Being honest helps us to avoid conduct we might be tempted to conceal

---

6. Why do marriage mates need to be honest with each other, and what dangers do they thus avoid?
7, 8. What Bible examples can help children to learn the value of honesty?

⁸ On the positive side, there are such accounts as that of Jacob, who urged his sons to return money they found in their bags because he felt that it might have been put there by mistake; that of Jephthah and his daughter, who honored her father's vow at great personal sacrifice; and that of Jesus, who bravely identified himself before a vicious mob in order to fulfill prophecy and protect his friends. (Genesis 43:12; Judges 11:30-40; John 18: 3-11) This partial list may give parents a taste of the riches found in God's Word that can help them teach their children to love and value honesty.

⁹ Such teaching places an important obligation on parents. The apostle Paul asked: "Do you, however, the one teaching someone else, not teach yourself? You, the one preaching 'Do not steal,' do you steal?" (Romans 2:21) Some parents confuse their children by teaching about honesty while acting dishonestly themselves. They may justify petty theft and deceptive words with such excuses as "Oh, they expect people to take these things" or "That was just a little white lie, a fib." In reality, stealing is stealing, regardless of the value of the item stolen, and lying is lying, regardless of the subject matter or the scope of the untruth.* (Luke 16:10) Children are quick to detect hypocrisy and may be seriously damaged by it. (Ephesians 6:4) However, when they learn honesty from their parents' examples, they may well grow up to glorify Jehovah in this dishonest world.—Proverbs 22:6.

---

* In the congregation setting, a practice of flagrant, malicious lying —clearly intended to hurt others—may warrant judicial action on the part of the elders.

9. What should parents avoid if they want to set an example of honesty for their children, and why is such an example important?

SATANIC LIES REGARDING SERIOUS SINS

When it comes to serious sins, there are some dangerous lies that Satan would love for you to believe. Happily, Christians are not ignorant of the Devil's "crafty acts." (Ephesians 6:11, footnote) Consider three of such lies.

"Sins can be hidden." In truth, Jehovah sees everything that we do. "All things are naked and openly exposed to the eyes of him with whom we have an accounting." (Hebrews 4:13) Since Jehovah knows the facts and since we have an accounting with him, why add to our guilt by attempting to hide a serious sin from his human servants?—See also 2 Samuel 12:12.

"The elders cannot be trusted, so don't tell them anything." Wicked King Ahab addressed Elijah this way: "O enemy of mine." (1 Kings 21: 20) As Jehovah's prophet in Israel, Elijah could have helped Ahab gain forgiveness. In the Christian congregation, Jesus provides the elders as "gifts in men." (Ephesians 4:8) Though imperfect, the elders are "keeping watch over [our] souls," that is, looking out for our spiritual health and welfare. (Hebrews 13:17) They are not the enemy; they are Jehovah's means of helping us.

"You protect a friend by helping him to conceal his sins." The truth is, we would do a sinner great harm by helping to conceal his sins. Serious sins are signs of real spiritual illness; concealing them is like hiding serious symptoms from a qualified doctor. (James 5:14, 15) The sinner may fear the possibility of discipline; but discipline is an expression of Jehovah's love, and it may well save the sinner's life. (Proverbs 3:12; 4:13) Furthermore, the persistent sinner likely presents a real danger to others in the congregation. Would you want to assist in the spread of his wrong attitudes that led him into sin? (Leviticus 5:1; 1 Timothy 5:22) By all means, then, make sure that the erring one brings the matter to the attention of the congregation elders.

HONESTY IN THE CONGREGATION

[10] Associating with fellow Christians affords us many opportunities to develop honesty. As we learned in Chapter 12, we need to be careful in the way we use the gift of speech, particularly among our spiritual brothers and sisters. Casual talk can so easily turn into harmful gossip, even slander! If we repeat a story of uncertain origin, we may be helping to spread a lie, so it is much better to keep our lips in check. (Proverbs 10:19) On the other hand, we may know something to be true, but that does not mean that it is worth saying. For example, the matter may be none of our business, or it may be unkind to speak about it. (1 Thessalonians 4:11) Some people excuse rudeness by calling it honesty, but our words should always be gracious and kind.—Colossians 4:6.

[11] It is particularly important that we be honest with those taking the lead in the congregation. Some who become involved in serious wrongdoing compound the

---

10. Regarding honest communication among fellow believers, what cautions do we need to keep in mind?
11, 12. (a) In what ways do some who become involved in serious wrongdoing compound the problem? (b) What are some lies that Satan promotes regarding serious sins, and how may we combat them? (c) How can we show ourselves honest with Jehovah's organization?

problem by trying to cover up their sin and lying to congregation elders when asked about it. Such ones even begin to lead a double life, pretending to serve Jehovah while pursuing a course of serious sin. In effect, such a course turns a person's whole life into a lie. (Psalm 12:2) Others tell the elders part of the truth while concealing essential facts. (Acts 5:1-11) Such dishonesty often stems from believing in lies that Satan promotes.—See the box "Satanic Lies Regarding Serious Sins," on pages 164-5.

12 It is also important to be honest with Jehovah's organization when we answer questions in writing. For example, when we report our activity in the ministry, we are careful not to falsify the facts. Similarly, when we fill out an application for some privilege of service, we should never misrepresent the real state of our health or any other aspect of our record.—Proverbs 6:16-19.

13 Our honesty with fellow believers also extends to matters of business. At times, Christian brothers and sisters may engage in business dealings together. They should be careful to keep such matters separate from the worship they carry out together at the Kingdom Hall or in the ministry. The business relationship may be that of an employer and an employee. If we employ brothers or sisters, we would be careful to treat them honestly, paying them in a timely way, in the amount agreed upon, and with the benefits arranged for or required by law. (1 Timothy 5:18; James 5:1-4) Conversely, if we are employed by a brother or a sister, we give the full amount of work for our wages. (2 Thessalonians 3:10) We do not expect preferential treatment because of

---

13. How can we maintain honesty if we have a business relationship with a fellow believer?

HOW HONEST AM I?

Principle: "O Jehovah, who will be a guest in your tent? . . . He who is walking faultlessly and practicing righteousness and speaking the truth in his heart."—Psalm 15:1, 2.

Some questions to ask yourself

■ Why is it important that I always speak the truth?—Proverbs 6:16, 17.

■ How can I "put away falsehood" when completing forms, such as school examination papers, tax returns, or government documents?—Ephesians 4:25; Isaiah 28:15; Matthew 22:17-21; Romans 13:1-7.

■ How are both my speech and my actions involved in my being an honest employee?—Proverbs 11:1; Ephesians 4:28; Colossians 3:9, 10.

■ If I develop a love of money, how could that love undermine my efforts to be truthful?—Psalm 37:21; 1 Timothy 6:9, 10.

our spiritual relationship, as if our employer owes us time off, benefits, or other advantages not accorded to other employees.—Ephesians 6:5-8.

¹⁴ What if our business involves some kind of joint venture, perhaps an investment or a loan? The Bible provides an important and useful principle: Put everything down in writing! For example, when Jeremiah bought a plot of land, he had a document made out in duplicate, duly witnessed, and safely stored for future reference. (Jeremiah 32:9-12; see also Genesis 23:16-20.) When doing business with fellow believers, putting all the details into a carefully prepared, signed, and witnessed document does not imply distrust. Rather, it helps to prevent misunderstandings, disappointments, and even divisive disagreements from arising. Any Christians doing business together should keep in mind that no business venture is ever worth endangering the unity and peace of the congregation.*—1 Corinthians 6:1-8.

HONESTY IN THE SECULAR WORLD

¹⁵ A Christian's honesty is not limited to the congregation. Paul said: "We wish to conduct ourselves honestly in *all* things." (Hebrews 13:18) When it comes to secular business matters, our Creator is very interested in honesty. In the book of Proverbs alone, there are four references to false scales. (Proverbs 11:1; 16:11; 20:10, 23) In ancient times, it was common to use scales and weights

---

* Regarding what to do should a business arrangement go wrong, consult the Appendix, pages 222-3.

---

14. When Christians engage in a joint business venture, what precaution do they wisely take, and why?
15. How does Jehovah feel about dishonest business practices, and how do Christians respond to such popular trends?

in business transactions in order to weigh out the goods purchased and the money used to purchase them. Dishonest merchants would use two sets of weights and an inaccurate scale to deceive and cheat their customers.* Jehovah hates such practices! To remain in his love, we strictly avoid any and all dishonest business practices.

16 Because Satan is the ruler of this world, we are not surprised to find that dishonesty is all around us. Daily we may face temptations to be dishonest. When people write up a résumé to apply for work, it is a common practice to lie and exaggerate, inventing credentials and falsifying experience. When people fill out forms for immigration, taxation, insurance, and the like, they commonly give false answers in order to get what they want. Many students cheat on tests, or when they write papers and reports for school, they may go to the Internet and plagiarize what they find there, falsely presenting someone else's work as their own. And when people deal with corrupt officials, they often offer bribes to get what they want. We expect as much in a world where so many are "lovers of themselves, lovers of money, . . . without love of goodness."—2 Timothy 3:1-5.

17 True Christians are resolved not to engage in any of those practices. What makes honesty a challenge at times is that those who do engage in such dishonest ways seem to succeed and even get ahead in today's world. (Psalm 73:1-8) Meanwhile, Christians may suffer

---

* They used one set of weights for buying and another for selling, favoring themselves either way. They might also use a scale with one arm longer or heavier than the other so that they could cheat the customer on any transaction.

16, 17. What forms of dishonesty are common in today's world, and what are true Christians resolved to do?

financially because they wish to remain honest "in *all* things." Is it worth the sacrifices involved? Absolutely! But why? What blessings result from honest conduct?

THE BLESSINGS OF BEING HONEST

¹⁸ There are few things you will ever find in life that are more valuable than a reputation as an honest, trustworthy person. (See the box "How Honest Am I?" on page 167.) And think of it—anyone can build such a reputation! It does not depend on your talent, wealth, looks, social background, or any other factor beyond your control. Nonetheless, many fail to acquire the treasure of a good reputation. It is a rarity. (Micah 7:2) Some may scoff at you for being honest, but others will appreciate your honesty, and they will reward you with their trust and their respect. Many of Jehovah's Witnesses have even found that their honesty benefited them financially. They have kept their jobs when dishonest employees were fired, or they have found a job when honest employees were desperately needed.

¹⁹ Whether that happens to you or not, you will find that honesty brings even greater blessings. You will have the blessing of a clean conscience. Paul wrote: "We trust we have an honest conscience." (Hebrews 13:18) Furthermore, your reputation never goes unnoticed by our loving heavenly Father, and he loves honest people. (Psalm 15:1, 2; Proverbs 22:1) Yes, being honest helps you to remain in God's love, and we seek no higher reward than that. Let us next consider a related subject: Jehovah's view of work.

---

18. Why is a reputation for honesty of great value?
19. How can a life course of honesty affect our conscience and our relationship with Jehovah?

CHAPTER 15

See Good for Your Hard Work

"Every man should . . . see good for all his hard work."—ECCLESIASTES 3:13.

FOR many people in today's world, work is anything but a pleasure. Laboring long hours at a job that they do not particularly enjoy, they dread going to work each day. How can those with such a mind-set be motivated to take a personal interest in their work—let alone find satisfaction in their job?

² The Bible promotes a positive view of hard work. It says that work and its fruitage are a blessing. Solomon wrote: "Every man should eat and indeed drink and see good for all his hard work. It is the gift of God." (Ecclesiastes 3:13) Jehovah, who loves us and always has our best interests at heart, wants us to find satisfaction in our work and to enjoy the fruits of our labor. To remain in his love, we need to live in harmony with his viewpoint and his principles regarding work.—Ecclesiastes 2:24; 5:18.

³ In this chapter, we will consider four questions: How can we see good for our hard work? What types of work are not for true Christians? How can we balance secular work with spiritual activities? And what is the most important work that we can do? First, though, let us

---

1-3. (a) How do many people feel about their job? (b) What view of work does the Bible promote, and what questions will we consider in this chapter?

examine the example of the two greatest workers in the universe—Jehovah God and Jesus Christ.

THE SUPREME WORKER AND THE MASTER WORKER

⁴ Jehovah is the Supreme Worker. Genesis 1:1 states: "In the beginning God created the heavens and the earth." When God completed his creative work involving the earth, he pronounced the results "very good." (Genesis 1:31) In other words, he was fully satisfied with all his earthly work. Jehovah, "the happy God," no doubt found great joy in being a productive worker. —1 Timothy 1:11.

⁵ Our industrious God never stops working. Long after physical creation respecting the earth was completed, Jesus said: "My Father has kept working until now." (John 5:17) What has the Father been doing? From his heavenly realm, he certainly has kept active in guiding and caring for humankind. He has brought forth "a new creation," spirit-begotten Christians who will eventually rule with Jesus in heaven. (2 Corinthians 5:17) He has been working toward the fulfillment of his purpose for humans—that those who love him gain everlasting life in a new world. (Romans 6:23) Jehovah must be very pleased with the results of this work. Millions have responded to the Kingdom message, being drawn by God and adjusting their life to remain in his love.—John 6:44.

⁶ Jesus has a long record of working hard. In his prehuman existence, he served as God's "master worker" in the creation of all things "in the heavens and upon the earth." (Proverbs 8:22-31; Colossians 1:15-17) When

---

4, 5. How does the Bible indicate that Jehovah is a productive worker?

6, 7. What long record of working hard does Jesus have?

on earth, Jesus continued to be a hard worker. Early in life, he learned the building trade, becoming known as "the carpenter."* (Mark 6:3) This trade involves strenuous work and a variety of skills—especially so in the era before sawmills, supply stores, and power tools. Can you imagine Jesus going out to get his own lumber—perhaps even felling trees and hauling the wood to wherever he was working? Can you picture him constructing houses—preparing and installing the roof beams, making the doors, and even building some of the furniture? Jesus undoubtedly knew firsthand the satisfaction that comes from hard work skillfully done.

⁷ Jesus was an outstandingly diligent worker in carrying out his ministry. For three and a half years, he was intensely occupied with this all-important work. Wanting to reach as many people as possible, he used his days to the full, rising early and working on into the night. (Luke 21:37, 38; John 3:2) He journeyed "from city to city and from village to village, preaching and declaring the good news of the kingdom of God." (Luke 8:1) Jesus literally covered hundreds of miles, traveling on foot along dusty roads to take the message of the good news to people.

⁸ Did Jesus see good for his hard work in the ministry? Yes! He sowed seeds of Kingdom truth, leaving behind fields that were ripe for harvesting. Doing God's work brought Jesus such strength and sustenance that he was willing to forgo food for the sake of getting it

---

* The Greek word rendered "carpenter" is said to be "a general term for a worker in wood whether he worked on houses or furniture or any other type of wooden objects."

8, 9. How did Jesus see good for his hard work?

done. (John 4:31-38) Think about the satisfaction he must have felt when at the end of his earthly ministry he could truthfully report to his Father: "I have glorified you on the earth, having finished the work you have given me to do."—John 17:4.

[9] Surely Jehovah and Jesus are the foremost examples of ones who see good for their hard work. Our love for Jehovah moves us to "become imitators of God." (Ephesians 5:1) Our love for Jesus impels us to "follow his steps closely." (1 Peter 2:21) So let us now examine how we too can see good for our hard work.

HOW TO SEE GOOD FOR OUR HARD WORK

[10] Secular work has a place in the life of true Christians. We want to find satisfaction and a measure of contentment in our work, but this can be a real challenge if we find ourselves working at a secular job that is not to our liking. How is it possible to see good for our work under such circumstances?

[11] *By cultivating a positive attitude.* We cannot always change our circumstances, but we can change our attitude. Meditating on God's viewpoint can help us to cultivate a positive attitude toward work. For example, if you are a family head, reflect on the fact that your job, no matter how menial it may seem to be, enables you to provide material necessities for your family. Thus caring for your loved ones is no small matter in God's eyes. His Word says that one who fails to provide for his family "is worse than a person who has disowned Jehovah." (1 Timothy 5:8; footnote) Recognizing that your job is a means to an end—making it possible for you to carry out a God-

---

10, 11. What can help us to cultivate a positive attitude toward our job?

Applying Bible principles can help you to see good for your hard work

given responsibility—can help you to find in your work a measure of fulfillment and purpose that may elude your coworkers.

¹² *By being diligent and honest.* Working hard and learning how to do our job well can lead to blessings. Diligent, skillful workers are often highly valued by their employers. (Proverbs 12:24; 22:29) As true Christians, we must also be honest in our work—not stealing money, materials, or time from our employer. (Ephesians 4:28)

---

12. In what ways is it rewarding to be diligent and honest in our work?

As we saw in the preceding chapter, honesty is rewarding. An employee with a reputation for honesty is likely to be trusted. And whether our employer takes notice of our example as a hard worker or not, we can have the satisfaction that comes from having "an honest conscience" and knowing that we are pleasing the God we love.—Hebrews 13:18; Colossians 3:22-24.

[13] *By recognizing that our conduct can glorify God.* When we maintain a high standard of Christian conduct at our place of work, others are bound to notice this. With what result? We may thus "adorn the teaching of our Savior, God." (Titus 2:9, 10) Yes, our fine conduct can cause others to see the beauty of our way of worship, making it more attractive to them. Just think of how you would feel if a coworker responded to the truth because of your good example in the workplace! Most important, consider this: What could be more rewarding than knowing that your fine conduct glorifies Jehovah and makes his heart rejoice?—Proverbs 27:11; 1 Peter 2:12.

USING DISCERNMENT IN OUR CHOICE OF WORK

[14] The Bible does not spell out in detail what is acceptable and what is not when it comes to secular work. This does not mean that we can accept just any kind of employment no matter what it involves. The Scriptures can help us to choose productive, honest work that is pleasing to God while avoiding employment that would be displeasing to him. (Proverbs 2:6) When facing decisions about employment, there are two key questions for us to consider.

---

13. Our good example in the workplace may have what results?
14-16. When facing decisions about employment, what key questions do we need to consider?

> ### SHOULD I TAKE THE JOB?
>
> **Principle:** "Do all things for God's glory."
> —1 Corinthians 10:31.
>
> **Some questions to ask yourself**
>
> - Does the job involve activities that are directly condemned in God's Word?—Exodus 20:13-15.
> - Would doing the work make me an accomplice in a condemned practice?—Revelation 18:4.
> - Is the work simply a human service that in itself is not Scripturally objectionable?—Acts 14:16, 17.
> - What is the effect of doing the work; will it hurt the consciences of others? —Romans 14:19-22.
> - If I take up work in another country and leave my family behind, what might be the emotional and spiritual effects on my family?—Ephesians 5:28–6:4.

[15] *Would doing this particular work in itself constitute an act condemned in the Bible?* God's Word clearly condemns stealing, lying, and the making of idols. (Exodus 20:4; Acts 15:29; Ephesians 4:28; Revelation 21:8) We would reject any employment that required us to do such things. Our love for Jehovah would never allow us to accept a job that involves engaging in practices that violate God's commands.—1 John 5:3.

¹⁶ *Would doing this work clearly make us an accomplice in or a promoter of a wrong practice?* Consider an example. Working as a receptionist is not wrong in itself. What, though, if a Christian were offered such a job at an abortion clinic? Granted, his job assignment would not require him to help with the abortion procedures directly. Nevertheless, would not his regular work there support the operation of a clinic that exists to perform abortions—a practice that is contrary to God's Word? (Exodus 21:22-24) As lovers of Jehovah, we do not want to be closely linked with unscriptural practices.

¹⁷ Many employment issues can be resolved by carefully analyzing the answers to the two key questions

---

17. (a) What factors can we weigh in making decisions about employment? (See the box on page 177.) (b) How may our conscience help us to make decisions that please God?

We can show our love for Jehovah by giving the preaching work priority in our life

posed in paragraphs 15 and 16. In addition, there are some other factors that we do well to weigh when making decisions about employment.* We cannot expect the faithful slave class to establish rules that will cover every situation that may arise. Here is where discernment is needed on our part. As we learned in Chapter 2, we need to educate and train our conscience by studying how to apply God's Word in our daily life. With our "perceptive powers" thus trained "through use," our conscience can help us to make decisions that please God and enable us to remain in his love.—Hebrews 5:14.

KEEPING A BALANCED ATTITUDE TOWARD WORK

18 Maintaining spiritual balance is not easy in these "last days" with their "critical times hard to deal with." (2 Timothy 3:1) Finding a job and holding on to it can be a real challenge. As true Christians, we recognize the importance of working hard to provide for our family. But if we are not careful, pressure in the workplace or the world's infectious materialistic thinking could interfere with our spiritual pursuits. (1 Timothy 6:9, 10) Let us consider how we can keep our balance, making sure of "the more important things."—Philippians 1:10.

19 *Place your full trust in Jehovah.* (Proverbs 3:5, 6) Is he not worthy of such trust? After all, he cares for us. (1 Peter 5:7) He knows our needs better than we do, and his hand is never short. (Psalm 37:25) We therefore do well

---

* For a more detailed discussion of employment factors to consider, see *The Watchtower*, April 15, 1999, pages 28-30, and July 15, 1982, page 26.

---

18. Why is it not easy to maintain spiritual balance?
19. Why is Jehovah worthy of our full trust, and what does such trust help us to avoid?

> ### "MY DECISION LED TO A LIFE OF JOY AND CONTENTMENT"
>
> "I excelled in my studies and won a full scholarship to a well-respected private school in New York City. My father pressured me to apply to several prestigious universities. I was accepted by a few of them and even earned a scholarship to one of the most renowned universities in the United States. However, I turned the offer down for two reasons. I could foresee the moral dangers of living on campus away from home, and I had a strong desire to pioneer.
>
> "I have now been a regular pioneer for more than 20 years. I have kept myself busy in many avenues of the ministry—serving where the need is greater, helping with Kingdom Hall construction, and assisting with disaster relief work. Currently, I have the pleasure of serving with a foreign-language group in New York City.
>
> "Looking back on my career in full-time service, I realize how blessed I have been. My decision led to a life of joy and contentment. I wouldn't exchange the experiences I've had and the friendships I've made for anything."—Zenaida.

to listen when his Word reminds us: "Let your manner of life be free of the love of money, while you are content with the present things. For [God] has said: 'I will by no means leave you nor by any means forsake you.'" (Hebrews 13:5) Many full-time servants can testify to God's ability to provide life's necessities. If we fully trust that Jehovah will care for us, we will avoid becoming unduly anxious about providing for our family. (Matthew 6:25-32) We will not allow secular work to cause us to neglect spiritual activities, such as preaching the good news and attending meetings.—Matthew 24:14; Hebrews 10:24, 25.

[20] *Keep your eye simple.* (Matthew 6:22, 23) Having a simple eye means keeping our life uncomplicated. A Christian's simple eye focuses on a single purpose—the doing of God's will. If our eye is properly focused, we will not be obsessed with chasing after a high-paying job and a more elaborate lifestyle. Neither will we get caught up in the never-ending quest for the latest and best material things that advertisers would have us believe we need in order to be happy. How can you maintain a simple eye? Avoid burdening yourself with unnecessary debt. Do not clutter your life with possessions that consume inordinate amounts of time and attention. Heed the Bible's counsel to be content with "sustenance and covering." (1 Timothy 6:8) Seek to simplify your life as much as possible.

[21] *Set spiritual priorities, and stick to them.* Since we can do only so much in life, we need to establish priorities. Otherwise, less important things could swallow up precious time, crowding out the more important things. What should have top priority in our life? Many in the world place primary emphasis on pursuing higher education in order to have a lucrative career in this system. Jesus, however, urged his followers to "keep on . . . seeking first the kingdom." (Matthew 6:33) Yes, as true Christians, we put God's Kingdom first in our life. Our pattern of life—the choices we make, the goals

---

20. What does it mean to keep a simple eye, and how can you maintain such an outlook?
21. Why do we need to establish priorities, and what should come first in our life?

WORKING HARD IN THE MINISTRY

²² Knowing that we are living deep in the time of the end, we keep focused on the main work of true Christians—preaching and disciple making. (Matthew 24:14; 28:19, 20) Like our Exemplar, Jesus, we want to be intensely occupied with this lifesaving work. How can we show that this work is important to us? The majority of God's people devote themselves to the preaching work wholeheartedly as congregation publishers. Some have arranged their affairs to serve as pioneers or missionaries. Recognizing the importance of spiritual goals, many parents have encouraged their children to pursue a career in the full-time service. Do zealous Kingdom proclaimers see good for their hard work in the ministry? Indeed, they do! Serving Jehovah whole-souled is the sure way to a life of joy, satisfaction, and countless blessings.—Proverbs 10:22.

²³ Many of us have to spend long hours in secular work to provide materially for our family. Remember that Jehovah wants us to see good for our hard work. By bringing our attitude and actions into harmony with his viewpoint and principles, we can find satisfaction in our work. Let us, however, be determined never to allow secular work to distract us from our main work—that of declaring the good news of God's Kingdom. By giving this work priority in our life, we show our love for Jehovah and thereby remain in his love.

22, 23. (a) What is the main work of true Christians, and how can we show that this work is important to us? (See the box on page 180.) (b) What is your determination regarding secular work?

CHAPTER 16

Oppose the Devil and His Crafty Acts

"Oppose the Devil, and he will flee."
—JAMES 4:7.

IF YOU have been serving Jehovah for decades, you have likely heard numerous baptism talks at our assemblies and conventions. Yet, no matter how often you have been present on such occasions, you likely still feel moved each time you witness the moment that those sitting in the front rows of the auditorium stand up to present themselves for baptism. At that instant, a buzz of excitement ripples through the audience, followed by a burst of heartfelt applause. Tears may well up in your eyes as you look at yet another group of precious individuals who have taken sides with Jehovah. What joy we feel at such times!

² While we may witness baptisms a few times a year in our locality, the angels are privileged to observe them much more often. Can you imagine how much "joy in heaven" there must be as they see thousands of individuals worldwide added to the visible part of Jehovah's organization each week? (Luke 15:7, 10) No doubt, the angels are thrilled to observe this increase!—Haggai 2:7.

THE DEVIL "WALKS ABOUT LIKE A ROARING LION"

³ In stark contrast, however, there are spirit creatures

1, 2. For whom are baptisms occasions for joy?
3. Why is Satan walking about "like a roaring lion," and what does he want to do?

who observe those baptisms with fury. For Satan and the demons, it is galling to see thousands turn their backs on this corrupt world. After all, Satan boasted that no humans serve Jehovah out of genuine love and that none would remain faithful under severe test. (Job 2:4, 5) Every time someone is moved to dedicate himself to Jehovah, Satan is proved wrong. It is as if Satan receives thousands of slaps in the face every week of the year. No wonder he "walks about like a roaring lion, seeking to devour someone"! (1 Peter 5:8) This "lion" is eager to devour us spiritually, causing us to damage or even sever our relationship with God.—Psalm 7:1, 2; 2 Timothy 3:12.

⁴ Although we face a fierce foe, we have no reason to

4, 5. (a) Jehovah has restricted Satan's influence in what two important ways? (b) Of what can a true Christian be assured?

Every time someone dedicates himself to Jehovah and is baptized, Satan is proved wrong

be overwhelmed by fear. Why not? Because Jehovah has restricted the reach of that "roaring lion" in two important ways. What are they? First of all, Jehovah has foretold that "a great crowd" of true Christians will survive the coming "great tribulation." (Revelation 7:9, 14) God's prophecies never fail. Therefore, even Satan must know that God's people as a whole are beyond his reach.

⁵ The second restriction can be deduced from a basic truth spoken by one of God's faithful men of old. The prophet Azariah said to King Asa: "Jehovah is with you as long as you prove to be with him." (2 Chronicles 15:2; 1 Corinthians 10:13) Numerous recorded examples demonstrate that in the past, Satan always failed to devour any of God's servants who remained close to God. (Hebrews 11:4-40) Today, a Christian who stays close to God will be able to oppose and even conquer the Devil. In fact, God's Word assures us: "Oppose the Devil, and he will flee from you."—James 4:7.

"WE HAVE A WRESTLING . . . AGAINST THE WICKED SPIRIT FORCES"

⁶ Satan cannot win the war, so to speak, but he can make casualties of us as individuals if we let our guard down. Satan knows that he can devour us if he can weaken our bond with Jehovah. How does Satan try to achieve this? By attacking us intensely, personally, and cunningly. Let us consider these main strategies of Satan.

⁷ *Intense attacks.* The apostle John stated: "The whole world is lying in the power of the wicked one." (1 John 5:19) Those words contain a warning for all true Christians. Since Satan has already devoured the entire ungodly world of mankind, he can now focus on and intensify his

---

6. How does Satan fight against individual Christians?
7. Why is Satan intensely attacking Jehovah's people?

attacks on those who have so far eluded him—Jehovah's people. (Micah 4:1; John 15:19; Revelation 12:12, 17) He has great anger because he knows his time is short. So he has stepped up the pressure. Today, we face his final rampage of savagery and destruction. Hence, now more than ever, we need to "discern the times to know what [we] ought to do."—1 Chronicles 12:32.

⁸ *Personal wrestling.* The apostle Paul warned fellow Christians: "We have a wrestling . . . against the wicked spirit forces in the heavenly places." (Ephesians 6:12) Why did Paul use the term "wrestling"? Because it conveys the idea of hand-to-hand combat and a struggle at close quarters. Thus, by using that term, Paul stressed that each of us has a personal fight with wicked spirits. Whether we live in a country where belief in wicked spirits is prevalent or not, we should never forget that when we dedicated ourselves to Jehovah, we stepped on the wrestling mat, as it were. At least from dedication onward, each Christian is locked in combat. No wonder that Paul saw the need to urge Christians in Ephesus three times to "stand firm"!—Ephesians 6:11, 13, 14.

⁹ *Cunning schemes.* Paul exhorts Christians to stand firm against Satan's "crafty acts." (Ephesians 6:11, footnote) Note Paul's use of the plural. Wicked spirits use not one but various cunning devices—and for good reason. In the course of time, some believers who have stood firm against one kind of trial have given in when faced with another. Hence, the Devil and the demons closely observe

---

8. What does the apostle Paul mean when he states that we have "a wrestling" against wicked spirits?
9. (a) Why do Satan and the demons employ various "crafty acts"? (b) Why does Satan try to corrupt our thinking, and how can we resist his efforts? (See the box on pages 192-3.) (c) Which crafty act will we now consider?

the behavior of each one of us to detect our weakest spot. Then they exploit any spiritual weakness we may have. Thankfully, though, we can recognize many of the Devil's methods, for they are revealed in the Bible. (2 Corinthians 2:11) Earlier in this publication, we discussed such schemes as the lure of materialism, harmful association, and sexual immorality. Let us now consider yet another one of Satan's crafty acts—spiritism.

PRACTICING SPIRITISM—AN ACT OF BETRAYAL

10 By practicing spiritism, or demonism, one makes direct contact with wicked spirits. Divination, sorcery, binding with spells, and inquiring of the dead are some forms of spiritism. As we well know, Jehovah views spiritism as "something detestable." (Deuteronomy 18:10-12; Revelation 21:8) Since we too must "abhor what is wicked," it is unthinkable that we would ever seek out the company of wicked spirit forces. (Romans 12:9) What a repulsive act of betrayal against our heavenly Father, Jehovah, that would be!

11 However, for the very reason that dabbling in spiritism is gross treachery against Jehovah, Satan is bent on getting some of us involved in it. Each time he can induce a Christian to turn to demonism, Satan scores a grand victory. Why? Think of this comparison: If a soldier could be persuaded to desert and betray his army unit and join enemy forces, the enemy commander would be delighted. He might even parade the traitor as a trophy, so as to insult that soldier's former army commander. Similarly, if a Christian turned to spiritism,

---

10. (a) What is spiritism? (b) How does Jehovah view spiritism, and how do you view it?
11. Why would it be a grand victory for Satan if he could induce us to turn to spiritism? Illustrate.

he would willingly and knowingly desert Jehovah and place himself directly under Satan's command. Imagine what pleasure it would give Satan to parade that deserter as a trophy of war! Would any of us want to hand the Devil such a victory? Absolutely not! We are not traitors.

RAISING QUESTIONS TO CREATE DOUBTS

[12] As long as we abhor spiritism, Satan will not succeed against us by using it. Hence, he realizes that he must change our thinking. How? He seeks ways to confuse Christians to the point that some will think that "good is bad and bad is good." (Isaiah 5:20) To do so, Satan often falls back on one of his time-tested methods—he raises questions to create doubts.

[13] Notice how Satan used that approach in the past. In Eden he asked Eve: *"Is it really so* that God said you must not eat from every tree of the garden?" In Job's time, during a meeting of the angels in heaven, Satan raised the question: *"Is it for nothing* that Job has feared God?" And at the start of Jesus' earthly ministry, Satan challenged Christ by saying: *"If you are* a son of God, tell these stones to become loaves of bread." Imagine—in Jesus' case, Satan dared to mock the very words that Jehovah himself had spoken some six weeks earlier: "This *is* my Son, the beloved, whom I have approved"!—Genesis 3:1; Job 1:9; Matthew 3:17; 4:3.

[14] Today, the Devil uses a similar scheme in an effort to create uncertainties about the wickedness of spiritism. Sadly, he has succeeded in raising doubts in the minds

---

12. What method does Satan use to influence our view of spiritism?
13. How has Satan used the method of raising questions to create doubts?
14. (a) How does Satan use his scheme of creating uncertainties regarding spiritism? (b) What will we now consider?

of some believers. They have begun to question whether certain forms of spiritism are truly all that evil. In effect, they are thinking, *'Is it really so?'* (2 Corinthians 11:3) How can we help such ones to adjust their thinking? How can we make sure that Satan's scheme fails to influence us? To answer, let us consider two areas of life that Satan has slyly contaminated with spiritistic elements. They are entertainment and health care.

EXPLOITING OUR DESIRES AND NEEDS

15 Especially in the Western world, occultism, witchcraft, and other forms of spiritism are taken more and more lightly. Movies, books, TV programs, and computer games increasingly portray demonistic practices as being fun, smart, and harmless. Some movies and books with plots focusing on the occult have become so wildly popular that devotees have organized fan clubs. Clearly, the demons have succeeded in trivializing the dangers of the occult. Has this trend of taking spiritism lightly influenced Christians? The thinking of some has been affected. In what way? To give a typical example, after one Christian watched a movie that centered on the occult, he said, "I saw the movie, but I didn't *practice* spiritism." Why is such reasoning dangerous?

16 Although there is a difference between actually practicing spiritism and watching it, that surely does not mean that watching occult practices poses no danger. Why not? Consider this: God's Word indicates that neither Satan nor his demons have the ability to read our

---

15. (a) How do many in the Western world view spiritism? (b) How have some Christians been influenced by the world's view of spiritism?
16. Why is it dangerous to choose entertainment that centers on occult practices?

thoughts.* Thus, as mentioned earlier, to find out what we are thinking and to detect any spiritual weakness in us, wicked spirits have to observe closely our actions—including our choice of entertainment. When a Christian's behavior shows that he enjoys movies or books that center on spirit mediums, magic spells, acts of demon possession, or similar demonistic subjects, he is sending a message to the demons. In effect, he is alerting them to his weak spot! In response, the demons could intensify their wrestling with that Christian in order to exploit the weakness he has revealed until they have pinned him down, so to speak. In fact, some whose interest in spiritism was first piqued by entertainment that prominently featured the occult have eventually become involved in actually practicing spiritism.—Galatians 6:7.

17 Satan tries to exploit not only our desire for entertainment but also our need for health care. How? A Christian whose health is failing despite numerous efforts to find a cure may become despondent. (Mark 5: 25, 26) That can provide Satan and the demons with a favorable opportunity to exploit him. They well know that God's Word warns against seeking "the assistance of those practicing what is hurtful." (Isaiah 31:2) To make a Christian go against that warning, the demons may tempt an ailing one to turn in desperation to treatments or procedures that involve the use of "uncanny power," or spiritism—something very hurtful. If that crafty act of

---

* The descriptive names given to Satan (Resister, Slanderer, Deceiver, Tempter, Liar) do not imply that he has the ability to search our hearts and minds. By way of contrast, however, Jehovah is described as "the examiner of hearts," and Jesus, as the one who "searches the kidneys and hearts."—Proverbs 17:3; Revelation 2:23.

---

17. By means of what crafty act may Satan exploit those who are ailing?

the demons succeeds, it could weaken the ailing one's relationship with God. In what way?

[18] Jehovah warned the Israelites who had resorted to "uncanny power": "When you spread out your palms, I hide my eyes from you. Even though you make many prayers, I am not listening." (Isaiah 1:13, 15) Of course, we always want to avoid anything that might hinder our prayers and diminish the support that we receive from Jehovah—and all the more so during a period of illness. (Psalm 41:3) Hence, if there are indications that a certain diagnostic procedure or therapeutic treatment may contain spiritistic elements, a true Christian should reject it.* (Matthew 6:13) In that way, he will be sure to retain Jehovah's backing.—See the box "Is It Really Spiritism?" on page 194.

Benefit from Jehovah's support in times of illness

WHEN STORIES ABOUT DEMONS ABOUND

[19] Whereas many people in Western lands make light of the danger of Satan's power, the opposite occurs in

---

* For further information, see the article "A Health Test for You?" in the December 15, 1994, issue of *The Watchtower,* pages 19-22, and the article "The Bible's Viewpoint: Your Choice of Medical Treatment —Does It Matter?" in the January 8, 2001, issue of *Awake!*

18. What types of procedures would a Christian reject, and why?
19. (a) The Devil has fooled many people into believing what about his power? (b) What stories should true Christians avoid?

BEWARE OF SATAN'S CUNNING!

Satan, a master of deception, has "blinded the minds of the unbelievers" for thousands of years now. (2 Corinthians 4:4) He has also been relentless in his efforts to corrupt the thinking of God's worshippers. Why? Satan understands that how we think affects the way we act. He knows that if he can distort our thinking, he can influence our actions for bad.—James 1:14, 15.

Remember Satan's method of misleading Eve. The apostle Paul wrote: "I am afraid that somehow, as the serpent seduced Eve by its cunning, your minds might be corrupted away from . . . the Christ." (2 Corinthians 11:3) Working through a cautious serpent, Satan seduced Eve into following a disastrous course. He sought to corrupt her mind, to warp her thinking. The tactic worked. Because she listened, her viewpoint changed, and what was unlawful became desirable. Once her mind was corrupted, she was easily drawn into a sinful act.—Genesis 3:1-6; Revelation 12:9.

Satan has not changed. His basic tenet remains the same: Corrupt the mind, and sinful actions will follow. Satan has this system's politics, religion, commerce, and entertainment set up to spread his propaganda. (John 14:30) He has succeeded in distorting the thinking of the vast majority of mankind, changing their attitudes and viewpoints. Conduct that was once viewed as sinful—such as practicing homosexuality, living together without marriage, and bearing children out of wedlock—is often viewed as acceptable, even desirable. How effective has Satan been in seducing humans? The Bible says: "The whole world is lying in the power of the wicked one."—1 John 5:19.

As Christians, we are by no means immune to Satan's methods. (1 Corinthians 10:12) Knowing that his time is short, Satan has "great anger" and is especially intent on misleading God's people. (Revelation 12:12) If we are not careful, the subtle propaganda of Satan and the many "deceivers of the mind" that he uses can corrupt our thinking and seduce us into sin.—Titus 1:10.

For example, consider the world's view of marriage. The Bible teaches that marriage is sacred, involving a lasting commitment. (Matthew 19:5, 6, 9) This world's movies and television programs often portray marriage as a casual agreement that can easily be abandoned. As Christians, we need to beware that this satanic propaganda does not corrupt our thinking. Left unchecked, this influence could distort our viewpoint, weakening our commitment to our mate. Faced with marital problems, we might be tempted to look outside the marriage for understanding and support. Soon another person—perhaps a coworker or a fellow believer—might seem to offer emotional closeness. If we allow a romantic attachment to form, we may find ourselves drawn into a sinful act.

As another example, consider the spirit of independence that permeates Satan's world. Many are "headstrong, puffed up with pride." (2 Timothy 3:4) If such a spirit were to corrupt our thinking, our view of submission and obedience might become distorted. Infected by this spirit, a brother might chafe at counsel from the elders. (Hebrews 12:5) A sister might begin to question God's arrangement of headship.—1 Corinthians 11:3.

We can be thankful that Jehovah warns us about Satan's methods. (2 Corinthians 2:11) Let us be determined never to allow satanic propaganda to make inroads into our thinking. To remain in God's love, we need to keep our "minds fixed on the things above."—Colossians 3:2.

other parts of the world. There the Devil has fooled many into believing that he has more power than he really does have. Some people live, eat, work, and sleep in dread of wicked spirits. Stories about powerful acts of demons abound. Such stories are often told with relish; people are fascinated by them. Should we share in spreading such stories? No, servants of the true God avoid doing so for two important reasons.

[20] First, by circulating stories about the exploits of the demons, one promotes the interests of Satan. How so? God's Word confirms that Satan is capable of powerful works, but it also warns that he uses "lying signs" and "deception." (2 Thessalonians 2:9, 10) Since Satan is the archdeceiver, he knows how to influence the minds of those who are inclined toward spiritism and how to make

---

20. How could one, perhaps unwittingly, spread Satan's propaganda?

IS IT REALLY SPIRITISM?

Principle: "The works of the flesh are manifest, and they are . . . practice of spiritism, . . . divisions, sects . . . Those who practice such things will not inherit God's kingdom."
—Galatians 5:19-21.

Some questions to ask yourself

- Is any custom that I follow associated with false religious beliefs?—2 Corinthians 6:16, 17.
- Are any objects that I use directly related to spiritistic practices?—Acts 19:19.
- Does any medical treatment I seek involve some form of uncanny or magical power?—Leviticus 19:26.

them believe things that are not true. Such ones may sincerely believe that they saw and heard certain things and may relate their experiences as truth. In time, their stories become exaggerated by constant retelling. If a Christian were to spread such stories, he would, in effect, be doing the bidding of the Devil—"the father of the lie." He would be spreading Satan's propaganda.—John 8:44; 2 Timothy 2:16.

[21] Second, even if a Christian had some real encounters with wicked spirits in the past, he would refrain from repeatedly entertaining fellow believers with stories about such things. Why? We are admonished: "Look intently at the Chief Agent and Perfecter of our faith, Jesus." (Hebrews 12:2) Yes, we are to focus our attention on Christ, not Satan. It is noteworthy that while on earth, Jesus did not entertain his disciples with stories about wicked spirits, although he could have said much about what Satan could or could not do. Rather, Jesus focused on the Kingdom message. Therefore, in imitation of Jesus and the apostles, we want to center our conversations on "the magnificent things of God."—Acts 2:11; Luke 8:1; Romans 1:11, 12.

[22] True, Satan employs various crafty acts, including spiritism, to try to destroy our relationship with Jehovah. However, by abhorring what is wicked and clinging to what is good, we give the Devil no opportunity to weaken our resolve to reject spiritism in all its forms. (Ephesians 4:27) Imagine what great "joy in heaven" there will be if we continue to "stand firm against the [crafty acts] of the Devil" until he is no more!—Ephesians 6:11; footnote.

---

21. On what do we want to center our conversations?
22. How may we continue to contribute to "joy in heaven"?

CHAPTER 17

"Building Up Yourselves on Your Most Holy Faith"

"By building up yourselves on your most holy faith, . . . keep yourselves in God's love."—JUDE 20, 21.

YOU are hard at work on a building project. The construction has been going on for some time and will continue well into the future. So far, the work has been challenging yet fulfilling. Come what may, you are determined never to give up or slack off, for the quality of your work will affect your life, even your future. Why? Because the building under construction is you!

² The disciple Jude stressed the building work that we do on ourselves. When he urged Christians to "keep yourselves in God's love," he also revealed in the same passage the key to doing so: "By building up yourselves on your most holy faith." (Jude 20, 21) What are some ways that you can build yourself up, making your faith stronger so that you will remain in God's love? Let us focus on three aspects of the spiritual building project before you.

KEEP BUILDING FAITH IN JEHOVAH'S RIGHTEOUS REQUIREMENTS

³ First of all, we need to strengthen our faith in divine

1, 2. What building project are you involved in, and why is the quality of your work so important?
3-5. (a) Satan would like to mislead you into having what view of Jehovah's requirements? (b) What should be our viewpoint of God's requirements, and what effect should it have on how we feel? Illustrate.

law. In the course of studying this book, you have considered a number of Jehovah's righteous requirements regarding conduct. What is your view of them? Satan would like to mislead you into viewing Jehovah's laws, principles, and standards as restrictive, even oppressive. He has been using this tactic ever since it proved so effective way back in Eden. (Genesis 3:1-6) Will his tactic work on you? Much will depend on your point of view.

⁴ To illustrate: As you walk along in a pleasant park, you notice a sturdy high fence blocking off part of the grounds. The landscape beyond the fence looks inviting. At first, you might view the fence as a needless restriction of your freedom. As you look through it, though, you notice a ferocious lion stalking prey on the other side! Now you see the fence for what it is—a protection. Is there a dangerous predator stalking you right now? God's Word warns: "Keep your senses, be watchful. Your adversary, the Devil, walks about like a roaring lion, seeking to devour someone."—1 Peter 5:8.

⁵ Satan is a vicious predator. Because Jehovah does not want us to become Satan's prey, He has instituted laws to protect us from the many "crafty acts" of that wicked one. (Ephesians 6:11, footnote) So whenever we meditate on God's laws, we should see in them the love of our heavenly Father. Viewed in that light, God's laws are a source of security and joy. The disciple James wrote: "He who peers into the perfect law that belongs to freedom and who persists in it . . . will be happy in his doing it." —James 1:25.

⁶ Living by God's commandments is the best way to build up our faith in the Lawgiver and in the wisdom of

---

6. What is the best way to build faith in God's righteous laws and principles? Give an example.

his laws. For example, "the law of the Christ" includes Jesus' command to teach others "all the things [he has] commanded." (Galatians 6:2; Matthew 28:19, 20) Christians also take seriously the directive to keep on meeting together for worship and upbuilding association. (Hebrews 10:24, 25) God's commandments include, too, the exhortation to pray to Jehovah regularly and often and from the heart. (Matthew 6:5-8; 1 Thessalonians 5:17) As we live by such commands, we see ever more clearly what loving guidelines they provide. Obeying them brings us a measure of joy and satisfaction that we could never find elsewhere in this troubled world. As you meditate on how you have personally benefited by living in accord with God's laws, does not your faith in them get stronger?

[7] Some worry, at times, that it will be too hard to stick with Jehovah's laws as the years pass. They fear that somehow they may fail. If you ever feel that way, keep these words in mind: "I, Jehovah, am your God, the One teaching you to benefit yourself, the One causing you

---

7, 8. How does God's Word reassure those who worry that they may not be able to maintain a righteous course as the years pass?

to tread in the way in which you should walk. O if only you would actually pay attention to my commandments! Then your peace would become just like a river, and your righteousness like the waves of the sea." (Isaiah 48:17, 18) Have you ever paused to think about how reassuring those words are?

⁸ Jehovah here reminds us that we benefit ourselves by obeying him. He promises two blessings if we do so. First, our peace will be like a river—serene, abundant, ongoing. Second, our righteousness will be like the waves of the sea. If you stand on a beach and watch the waves roll in one after the other, you no doubt feel a sense of permanence. You know that the waves will keep coming, breaking on that beach for countless ages to come. Jehovah says that your righteousness—your course of doing right—can be like that. As long as you endeavor to be faithful to him, he will never let you fail! (Psalm 55:22) Do not such heartwarming promises build up your faith in Jehovah and in his righteous requirements?

"PRESS ON TO MATURITY"

⁹ A second aspect of your building project is revealed in these inspired words: "Let us press on to maturity." (Hebrews 6:1) Maturity is a wonderful goal for a Christian. Unlike perfection, which for now is beyond the reach of humans, maturity is an attainable goal. Further, Christians find greater joy in serving Jehovah as they mature. Why is that?

¹⁰ A mature Christian is a spiritual person. He looks at things from Jehovah's point of view. (John 4:23) Paul wrote: "Those who are in accord with the flesh set their minds on the things of the flesh, but those in accord

---

9, 10. (a) Why is maturity a wonderful goal for Christians? (b) How does a spiritual outlook contribute to joy?

with the spirit on the things of the spirit." (Romans 8:5) A fleshly outlook brings little joy, for it tends to be self-centered, shortsighted, and focused on material things. A spiritual outlook is joyous, for it is focused on Jehovah, "the happy God." (1 Timothy 1:11) A spiritual person is eager to please Jehovah and rejoices even when under trial. Why? Trials present opportunities to prove Satan a liar and to build integrity, delighting our heavenly Father.—Proverbs 27:11; James 1:2, 3.

¹¹ Spirituality and maturity come through training. Consider this verse: "Solid food belongs to mature people, to those who through use have their perceptive powers trained to distinguish both right and wrong." (Hebrews 5:14) When Paul spoke of our perceptive powers being "trained," he used a Greek word that was likely in common use in the gymnasiums of first-century Greece, for it can be rendered 'trained like a gymnast.' Now think of what such training involves.

¹² When we were born, our body was untrained. For example, a baby is barely able to perceive the orientation of its little limbs. Hence, a baby waves its arms randomly, even striking itself on the face, much to the baby's own dismay and surprise. Gradually, through use, the body is trained. The baby crawls, the toddler walks, the child runs.* Ah, but what about a gymnast? When

---

* Scientists say that we develop a special sense called proprioception, which is the body's sense of its own orientation and the placement of the limbs. For example, this sense enables you to clap your hands with your eyes closed. One adult patient who lost her proprioception was unable to stand, walk, or even sit up as a result.

11, 12. (a) What did Paul say about the "perceptive powers" of a Christian, and what is the meaning of the word rendered "trained"? (b) What training must the body undergo in order to mature and become physically adept?

A gymnast's body is trained through use

you see such an athlete vaulting and twisting through the air with exquisite grace and precision, there is no question in your mind that the body is like a finely tuned machine. The gymnast's expertise did not come about by accident—countless hours of training were required. Such bodily training, the Bible acknowledges, is "beneficial for a little." How much more valuable is the training of our spiritual perceptive powers!—1 Timothy 4:8.

[13] In this book, we have discussed much that will help you to train your perceptive powers so that you can remain faithful to Jehovah as a spiritual person. Prayerfully consider divine principles and laws as you make decisions in your day-to-day life. In every decision you face, ask yourself: 'What Bible laws or principles bear on this matter? How can I apply them? What course will please my heavenly Father?' (Proverbs 3:5, 6; James 1:5) Each decision you make in that way will further train your perceptive powers. Such training will help you to become and remain a truly spiritual person.

[14] While maturity is attainable, there is always room for spiritual growth. Growth is dependent on food. Paul thus noted: "Solid food belongs to mature people." A key to building up your faith is to keep taking in solid

---

13. How can we train our perceptive powers?
14. We need to acquire what appetite in order to grow spiritually, yet what caution do we need to keep in mind?

spiritual food. As you rightly apply what you learn, that is wisdom, and the Bible says: "Wisdom is the prime thing." Thus, we need to develop a genuine hunger for the precious truths our Father imparts. (Proverbs 4:5-7; 1 Peter 2:2) Of course, gaining knowledge and godly wisdom is no reason to become smug or haughty. We need to examine ourselves regularly lest pride or some other weakness takes root and grows in our heart. Paul wrote: "Keep testing whether you are in the faith, keep proving what you yourselves are."—2 Corinthians 13:5.

¹⁵ Construction of a house may be completed, yet work goes on. Maintenance and repairs are essential, and additions may be necessary as circumstances change. What do we need in order to mature and to maintain our spirituality? Above all, love. We need to keep growing in love for Jehovah and for our fellow believers. If we do not have love, all our knowledge and works would amount to nothing—like a lot of empty noise. (1 Corinthians 13:1-3) With love, we can attain Christian maturity and continue growing spiritually.

KEEP YOUR MIND FOCUSED ON THE HOPE JEHOVAH PROVIDES

¹⁶ Let us consider one more aspect of your building project. In order to build yourself up as a genuine follower of Christ, you need to guard the way you think. Satan, the ruler of this world, is a master at getting people to give in to negative thinking, pessimism, distrust, and despair. (Ephesians 2:2) Such thinking is as dangerous to a Christian as dry rot is to a wooden building. Happily, Jehovah provides a vital defensive tool—hope.

---

15. Why is love essential to spiritual growth?
16. Satan promotes what kind of thinking, and what defense has Jehovah provided?

¹⁷ The Bible lists the various parts of the suit of spiritual armor we need in our fight against Satan and this world. A prominent piece of the armor is the helmet, "the hope of salvation." (1 Thessalonians 5:8) A soldier in Bible times knew that he would not last long in battle without his helmet. Often made of metal and fitted over a cap of felt or leather, the helmet ensured that most blows directed at the head would glance off with little harm done. As a helmet protects the head, hope can protect your mind, your thinking.

¹⁸ Jesus set the prime example in maintaining hope. Remember what he endured on the final night of his life on earth. An intimate friend betrayed him for money. Another denied even knowing him. The others abandoned him and fled. His own countrymen turned against him, crying out for his death by torture at the hands of Roman soldiers. It seems safe to say that Jesus faced heavier trials than we will ever face. What helped him? Hebrews 12:2 answers: "For the joy that was set before him he endured a torture stake, despising shame, and has sat down at the right hand of the throne of God." Jesus never lost sight of "the joy that was set before him."

¹⁹ What joy was set before Jesus? Well, he knew that by enduring, he would contribute to the sanctification of Jehovah's holy name. He would provide the greatest possible proof that Satan is a liar. No hope could give Jesus greater joy! He knew, too, that Jehovah would richly reward his faithful course—that just ahead of him lay a wonderful time when he would be reunited with his Father. Jesus kept such a joyful hope in his mind

---

17. How does God's Word illustrate the importance of hope?
18, 19. Jesus set what example in maintaining hope, and how can we imitate him?

throughout the worst of times. We need to do the same. We too have joy set before us. Jehovah dignifies each of us with the privilege of helping to sanctify his great name. We can prove Satan a liar by choosing Jehovah as our Sovereign and keeping ourselves safe in the love of our Father no matter what trials and temptations we may face.

20 Jehovah is not just willing to reward his faithful servants—he is eager to do so. (Isaiah 30:18; Malachi 3:10) He delights in granting his servants the righteous desires of their heart. (Psalm 37:4) So keep your mind firmly focused on the hope that lies before you. Never give in to the negative, degraded, twisted thinking of Satan's old world. If you sense that the spirit of this world is making inroads into your mind or heart, pray fervently to Jehovah for "the peace of God that excels all thought." That God-given peace will guard your heart and your mental powers.—Philippians 4:6, 7.

21 What a thrilling hope you have to ponder! If you

---

20. What can help you to keep your thinking positive and hopeful?
21, 22. (a) What glorious hope do those of the "great crowd" cherish? (b) What part of the Christian hope means the most to you, and what is your resolve?

are part of the "great crowd," who will "come out of the great tribulation," think of the life that will soon open up before you. (Revelation 7:9, 14) With Satan and his demons out of the way, you will feel relief that may be hard to fathom now. Who of us, after all, has ever experienced life *without* the pressure of Satan's corrupting influence? With that pressure gone, what a joy it will be to work at transforming the earth into a paradise under the direction of Jesus and his 144,000 heavenly corulers! How we thrill at the prospect of seeing all sicknesses and infirmities done away with, of welcoming back our loved ones from the grave, of living life the way God meant us to live it! As we grow to perfection, an even greater reward will draw ever closer, the promise revealed at Romans 8:21—"the glorious freedom of the children of God."

[22] Jehovah wants you to attain a greater measure of freedom than you can even imagine. The path to that freedom lies in obedience. Is it not worth every effort you can put forth now to obey Jehovah day by day? By all means, then, keep building up yourself on your most holy faith, that you may remain in God's love for all eternity!

APPENDIX

TOPIC	PAGE

How to Treat a Disfellowshipped Person 207

Head Coverings—When and Why? 209

Flag Salute, Voting, and Civilian Service 212

Blood Fractions and Surgical Procedures 215

Gain the Victory Over Masturbation 218

The Bible's View on Divorce and Separation 219

Resolving Disputes in Business Matters 222

How to Treat a Disfellowshipped Person

Few things can hurt us more deeply than the pain we suffer when a relative or a close friend is expelled from the congregation for unrepentant sin. How we respond to the Bible's direction on this matter can reveal the depth of our love for God and of our loyalty to his arrangement.* Consider some questions that arise on this subject.

How should we treat a disfellowshipped person? The Bible says: "Quit mixing in company with anyone called a brother that is a fornicator or a greedy person or an idolater or a reviler or a drunkard or an extortioner, not even eating with such a man." (1 Corinthians 5:11) Regarding everyone that "does not remain in the teaching of the Christ," we read: "Never receive him into your homes or say a greeting to him. For he that says a greeting to him is a sharer in his wicked works." (2 John 9-11) We do not have spiritual or social fellowship with disfellowshipped ones. *The Watchtower* of September 15, 1981, page 25, stated: "A simple 'Hello' to someone can be the first step that develops into a conversation and maybe even a friendship. Would we want to take that first step with a disfellowshiped person?"

Is strict avoidance really necessary? Yes, for several reasons. First, it is a matter of loyalty to God and his Word. We obey Jehovah not only when it is convenient but also when doing so presents real challenges. Love for God moves us to obey all his commandments, recognizing that he is just and loving and that his laws promote the greatest good. (Isaiah 48:17; 1 John 5:3) Second, withdrawing from an unrepentant wrongdoer protects us and the rest of the congregation from spiritual and moral contamination and upholds the congregation's good name. (1 Corinthians 5:6, 7) Third, our

---

* Bible principles on this subject apply equally to those who disassociate themselves from the congregation.

firm stand for Bible principles may even benefit the disfellowshipped one. By supporting the decision of the judicial committee, we may touch the heart of a wrongdoer who thus far has failed to respond to the efforts of the elders to assist him. Losing precious fellowship with loved ones may help him to come "to his senses," see the seriousness of his wrong, and take steps to return to Jehovah.—Luke 15:17.

What if a relative is disfellowshipped? In such a case, the close bond between family members can pose a real test of loyalty. How should we treat a disfellowshipped relative? We cannot here cover every situation that may arise, but let us focus on two basic ones.

In some instances, the disfellowshipped family member may still be living in the same home as part of the immediate household. Since his being disfellowshipped does not sever the family ties, normal day-to-day family activities and dealings may continue. Yet, by his course, the individual has chosen to break the spiritual bond between him and his believing family. So loyal family members can no longer have spiritual fellowship with him. For example, if the disfellowshipped one is present, he would not participate when the family gets together to study the Bible. However, if the disfellowshipped one is a minor child, the parents are still responsible to instruct and discipline him. Hence, loving parents may arrange to conduct a Bible study with the child.*—Proverbs 6:20-22; 29:17.

In other cases, the disfellowshipped relative may be living outside the immediate family circle and home. Although there might be a need for limited contact on some rare occasion to care for a necessary family matter, any such contact should be kept to a minimum. Loyal Christian family

---

* For more information about disfellowshipped minor children living in the home, see *The Watchtower* of October 1, 2001, pages 16-17, and November 15, 1988, page 20.

members do not look for excuses to have dealings with a disfellowshipped relative not living at home. Rather, loyalty to Jehovah and his organization moves them to uphold the Scriptural arrangement of disfellowshipping. Their loyal course has the best interests of the wrongdoer at heart and may help him to benefit from the discipline received.*—Hebrews 12:11.

---

* For more information about how to treat disfellowshipped relatives, see the Scriptural counsel discussed in *The Watchtower* of April 15, 1988, pages 26-31, and September 15, 1981, pages 26-31.

Head Coverings—When and Why?

When and why should a Christian woman wear a head covering in connection with her worship? Let us consider the apostle Paul's inspired discussion of this subject. He provides the guidance we need in order to make good decisions, ones that honor God. (1 Corinthians 11:3-16) Paul reveals three factors to weigh: (1) the *activities* that call for a woman to wear such a covering, (2) the *settings* in which she should do so, and (3) the *motives* for her to apply this standard.

The activities. Paul mentions two: prayer and prophesying. (Verses 4, 5) Prayer, of course, is worshipful address to Jehovah. Today, prophesying would apply to any Bible-based teaching that a Christian minister does. Is Paul suggesting, though, that a woman should cover her head whenever she prays or teaches Bible truth? No. The setting in which a woman prays or teaches makes all the difference.

The settings. Paul's words suggest two settings, or spheres of activity—the family and the congregation. He says: "The head of a woman is the man . . . Every woman that prays or prophesies with her head uncovered shames her head." (Verses 3, 5) In the family arrangement, the woman's husband is the one whom Jehovah designates as her head.

Unless she gives due recognition to her husband's authority, she would shame her husband if she handled responsibilities that Jehovah assigns to him. For example, if it became necessary for her to conduct a Bible study in her husband's presence, she would acknowledge his authority by wearing a head covering. She would do so whether he is baptized or not, since he is the head of the family.* If she were to pray or to teach in the presence of her minor baptized son, she would likewise wear a head covering, not because he is the head of the family, but because of the authority granted to baptized male members of the Christian congregation.

Paul mentions the congregation setting, saying: "If any man seems to dispute for some other custom, we have no other, neither do the congregations of God." (Verse 16) In the Christian congregation, headship is given to baptized males. (1 Timothy 2:11-14; Hebrews 13:17) Only males are appointed as elders and ministerial servants with the God-given responsibility to care for the flock of God. (Acts 20:28) Occasionally, though, circumstances may require that a Christian woman be called on to handle a duty normally performed by a qualified baptized male. For instance, she may need to conduct a meeting for field service because a qualified baptized male is not available or present. Or she may conduct a prearranged home Bible study in the presence of a baptized male. Because such activities are really extensions of the Christian congregation, she would wear a head covering to acknowledge that she is handling the duty normally assigned to a male.

On the other hand, many aspects of worship do not call for a sister to wear a head covering. For example, she does not need to do so when commenting at Christian meetings, engaging in the door-to-door ministry with her husband

---

* A Christian wife would not normally pray aloud in the presence of her believing husband except in unusual circumstances, such as if he has been rendered mute by an illness.

or another baptized male, or studying or praying with her unbaptized children. Of course, other questions may arise, and if a sister is unsure about a matter, she may do additional research.* If still unsure and if her conscience moves her to do so, wearing a head covering would not be wrong.

The motives. In verse 10, we find two reasons why a Christian woman would want to fulfill this requirement: "The woman ought to have a sign of authority upon her head because of the angels." First, note the expression, "a sign of authority." Wearing a head covering is a way for a woman to show that she acknowledges the authority that Jehovah has placed upon baptized males in the congregation. Hence, she expresses her love for and loyalty to Jehovah God. A second reason is found in the words "because of the angels." How does a woman affect those mighty spirit creatures by wearing a head covering?

The angels are interested in seeing that divine authority is recognized throughout Jehovah's organization, in heaven and on earth. They also benefit from the examples of imperfect humans in this regard. After all, they too have to be submissive to Jehovah's arrangement—a test that more than a few angels failed in times past. (Jude 6) Now, the angels may see instances when a Christian woman is more experienced, more knowledgeable, and more intelligent than a baptized male in the congregation; yet, she readily shows her submission to his authority. In some cases, the woman is an anointed Christian who will later become one of

---

* For more information, please see *The Watchtower,* July 15, 2002, pages 26-7, and February 15, 1977, pages 125-8.

Christ's joint heirs. Such a woman will eventually serve in a position even higher than that enjoyed by angels and rule with Christ in heaven. What a fine example for the angels to observe now! Really, what a privilege all sisters have to demonstrate humble obedience through their loyal and submissive conduct in the sight of millions of faithful angels!

Flag Salute, Voting, and Civilian Service

Flag salute. Jehovah's Witnesses believe that bowing down to a flag or saluting it, often in conjunction with an anthem, is a religious act that ascribes salvation, not to God, but to the State or to its leaders. (Isaiah 43:11; 1 Corinthians 10:14; 1 John 5:21) One such leader was King Nebuchadnezzar of ancient Babylon. To impress the people with his majesty and religious ardor, this powerful monarch erected a great image and compelled his subjects to bow down to it while music, like an anthem, was being played. However, three Hebrews—Shadrach, Meshach, and Abednego—refused to bow to the image, even on pain of death.—Daniel, chapter 3.

In our age, "nationalism's chief symbol of faith and central object of worship is the flag," wrote historian Carlton Hayes. "Men bare their heads when the flag passes by; and in praise of the flag poets write odes and children sing hymns." Nationalism, he added, also has its "holy days," such as the Fourth of July in the United States, as well as its "saints and heroes" and its "temples," or shrines. In a public ceremony in Brazil, the minister general of the army acknowledged: "The flag is venerated and worshiped . . . just as the Fatherland is worshiped." Yes, "the flag, like the cross, is sacred," *The Encyclopedia Americana* once observed.

The aforementioned encyclopedia more recently noted that national anthems "are expressions of patriotic feeling and often include an invocation for divine guidance and protection of the people or their rulers." Jehovah's servants are not being unreasonable, therefore, when they view patriotic ceremonies involving the flag salute and national anthems as religious. In fact, when commenting on the refusal of children of Jehovah's Witnesses to give homage to the flag or to swear the oath of allegiance in U.S. schools, the book *The American Character* stated: "That these daily rituals are religious has been at last affirmed by the Supreme Court in a series of cases."

While not joining in ceremonies that they view as unscriptural, Jehovah's people certainly respect the right of others to do so. They also respect national flags as emblems and recognize duly constituted governments as "superior authorities" serving as "God's minister." (Romans 13:1-4) Hence, Jehovah's Witnesses heed the exhortation to pray "concerning kings and all those who are in high station." Our motive, though, is "in order that we may go on leading a calm and quiet life with full godly devotion and seriousness."—1 Timothy 2:2.

Voting in political elections. True Christians respect the right of others to vote. They do not campaign against elections, and they cooperate with elected authorities. However, they remain resolutely neutral with regard to the political affairs of the nations. (Matthew 22:21; 1 Peter 3:16) What should a Christian do in lands where voting is compulsory or in a situation where feelings run high against those who do not go to the voting booth? Remembering that Shadrach, Meshach, and Abednego went as far as the plain of Dura, a Christian, under similar circumstances, may decide to go to the booth if his conscience permits. However, he will take care not to violate his neutrality. He should take into account the following six principles:

1. Jesus' followers are "no part of the world."—John 15:19.

2. Christians represent Christ and his Kingdom.—John 18:36; 2 Corinthians 5:20.

3. The Christian congregation is united in belief, and its members are bound together by Christlike love.—1 Corinthians 1:10; Colossians 3:14.

4. Those who elect a certain official share responsibility for what he does.—Note the principles behind the words recorded at 1 Samuel 8:5, 10-18 and 1 Timothy 5:22.

5. Jehovah viewed Israel's desire for a visible ruler as a sign that they had rejected Him.—1 Samuel 8:7.

6. Christians must have freeness of speech when speaking to people of all political persuasions about God's Kingdom government.—Matthew 24:14; 28:19, 20; Hebrews 10:35.

Civilian service. In some lands, the State requires that those who reject military service engage in some form of civilian service for a period of time. When faced with a decision on this matter, we should pray about it, perhaps discuss it with a mature fellow Christian, and then make our decision on the basis of an informed conscience.—Proverbs 2:1-5; Philippians 4:5.

God's Word tells us to "be obedient to governments and authorities as rulers, to be ready for every good work, . . . to be reasonable." (Titus 3:1, 2) With that in mind, we might ask ourselves the following questions: 'Will accepting the proposed civilian work compromise my Christian neutrality or cause me to be involved with false religion?' (Micah 4:3, 5; 2 Corinthians 6:16, 17) 'Would doing this work make it difficult for me to fulfill my Christian responsibilities or even prevent me from fulfilling them?' (Matthew 28:19, 20; Ephesians 6:4; Hebrews 10:24, 25) 'On the other hand, would engaging in such service involve a schedule that would allow me to expand my spiritual activities, perhaps sharing in the full-time ministry?'—Hebrews 6:11, 12.

If a Christian conscientiously concludes that he could perform civilian service rather than go to prison, fellow Christians should respect his decision. (Romans 14:10) If, though, he feels that he cannot perform such service, others should respect that position as well.—1 Corinthians 10:29; 2 Corinthians 1:24.

Blood Fractions and Surgical Procedures

Blood fractions. Fractions are derived from the four primary blood components—red cells, white cells, platelets, and plasma. For example, red cells contain the protein hemoglobin. Products developed from human or animal hemoglobin have been used to treat patients who have acute anemia or massive blood loss.

Plasma—which is 90 percent water—carries scores of hormones, inorganic salts, enzymes, and nutrients, including minerals and sugar. Plasma also carries clotting factors, antibodies to fight disease, and such proteins as albumin. If someone is exposed to a certain disease, doctors might prescribe injections of gamma globulin extracted from the plasma of people who already had immunity. White blood cells may be a source of interferons and interleukins, used to treat some viral infections and cancers.

Should Christians accept therapies incorporating blood fractions? The Bible does not give specific details, so each one must make his own conscientious decision before God. Some would refuse all fractions, reasoning that God's Law to Israel required that blood removed from a creature be "[poured] out upon the ground." (Deuteronomy 12:22-24) Others, while refusing transfusions of whole blood or its major components, might accept treatments involving a

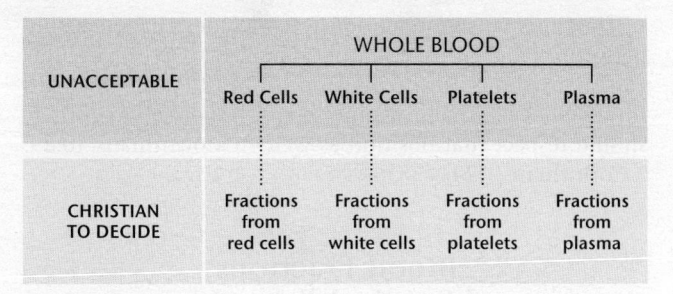

UNACCEPTABLE	WHOLE BLOOD			
	Red Cells	White Cells	Platelets	Plasma
CHRISTIAN TO DECIDE	Fractions from red cells	Fractions from white cells	Fractions from platelets	Fractions from plasma

fraction. They may reason that at some point fractions that have been extracted from blood cease to represent the life of the creature from which the blood was taken.

When making decisions about blood fractions, consider the following questions: Am I aware that refusing all blood fractions means that I will not accept some medications that include products to fight diseases or that might help the blood to clot in order to stop bleeding? Could I explain to a physician why I reject or accept the use of one or more blood fractions?

Surgical procedures. These include hemodilution and cell salvage. In hemodilution, blood is diverted from the body, replaced with a volume expander, and later returned to the patient. Cell salvage captures and returns blood lost during surgery. Blood is recovered from a wound or a body cavity, washed or filtered, and then reinfused into the patient. Because the methods of applying these techniques can vary from physician to physician, a Christian should find out what his doctor has in mind.

When making decisions about these procedures, ask yourself: 'If some of my blood will be diverted outside my body and the flow might even be interrupted for a time, will my conscience allow me to view this blood as still part of me, thus not requiring that it be "[poured] out upon the ground"? (Deuteronomy 12:23, 24) Would my Bible-trained conscience be troubled if during a medical procedure some of my own blood was withdrawn, modified, and directed back into my body? Am I aware that refusing all medical procedures involving the use of my own blood means that I would not accept a blood test, hemodialysis, or a heart-lung bypass machine?'

> ### SUGGESTED QUESTIONS FOR THE DOCTOR
>
> If you face surgery or a treatment that might involve a blood product, check that you have completed the appropriate legal documentation, such as a Health Care Proxy, which is designed to protect you from blood transfusion. In addition, you might ask your physician the following questions:
>
> ■ Do all the medical personnel involved know that as one of Jehovah's Witnesses, I direct that *no blood transfusions* (whole blood, red cells, white cells, platelets, or blood plasma) be given to me under any circumstances?
>
> ■ If a medicine containing blood fractions is recommended, what is its makeup? How much of this medicine might be administered, and in what way?
>
> ■ If my conscience permits me to accept a blood fraction, what are the medical risks? What alternate therapies are available?
>
> Before deciding on any of the foregoing, express your concerns to Jehovah in prayer. He promises to give the needed wisdom to all who "keep on asking" for it in faith.—James 1:5, 6.

A Christian must decide for himself how he will allow his own blood to be handled in the course of a surgical procedure. The same applies to medical tests and current therapies that involve extracting a small amount of one's own blood, perhaps modifying it in some way, and then reinjecting it.

Gain the Victory Over Masturbation

A spiritually unhealthy habit, masturbation instills attitudes that foster self-centeredness and corrupt the mind.* A masturbator may also grow to view others as mere sex objects—tools for sexual satisfaction. Sex becomes separated from love and is relegated to a reflex that gives momentary pleasure and relieves sexual tension. But that relief is only temporary. In reality, instead of deadening the body's members "as respects fornication, uncleanness, [and improper] sexual appetite," masturbation arouses them. —Colossians 3:5.

The apostle Paul wrote: "Beloved ones, let us cleanse ourselves of every defilement of flesh and spirit, perfecting holiness in God's fear." (2 Corinthians 7:1) If you are struggling to heed these words, do not give in to despair. Jehovah is always "ready to forgive" and to help. (Psalm 86:5; Luke 11:9-13) Indeed, your self-condemning heart and your efforts to give up the habit—despite occasional relapses—indicate a good attitude. Keep in mind, too, that "God is greater than our hearts and knows all things." (1 John 3:20) God sees more than our sins; he sees the whole person. This knowledge enables him to hear with sympathy our earnest pleas for mercy. So never weary of turning to God in hum-

---

* *Masturbation* is the stroking or rubbing of the genital organs, commonly resulting in orgasm.

ble and earnest prayer, like a child who goes to his father when in trouble. Jehovah will bless you with a cleansed conscience. (Psalm 51:1-12, 17; Isaiah 1:18) Of course, you need to take positive steps in harmony with your prayers. For example, you would strive to avoid all forms of pornography as well as bad associates.*

If your problem with masturbation persists, please speak about the matter with a Christian parent or a spiritually mature and caring friend.#—Proverbs 1:8, 9; 1 Thessalonians 5:14; Titus 2:3-5.

---

* As a practical step in controlling the use of a home computer, many families keep it in a public area. Additionally, some households purchase software that filters out undesirable material. No system, though, is completely reliable.

\# For practical suggestions on how to overcome masturbation, see the article "Young People Ask . . . How Can I Conquer This Habit?" in the November 2006 issue of *Awake!*, and pages 205-11 of the book *Questions Young People Ask—Answers That Work*, Volume 1.

The Bible's View on Divorce and Separation

Jehovah expects those who are married to remain faithful to the marriage vow. When uniting the first man and woman in marriage, Jehovah stated: "A man . . . must stick to his wife and they must become one flesh." Later, Jesus Christ repeated that statement and added: "Therefore, what God has yoked together let no man put apart." (Genesis 2:24; Matthew 19:3-6) Hence, Jehovah and Jesus view marriage as a lifelong bond that ends only when one partner dies. (1 Corinthians 7:39) Since marriage is a sacred arrangement, divorce is not to be taken lightly. In fact, Jehovah hates divorces that have no Scriptural basis.—Malachi 2:15, 16.

What forms a Scriptural basis for divorce? Well, Jehovah hates adultery and fornication. (Genesis 39:9; 2 Samuel 11:26, 27; Psalm 51:4) Indeed, he finds fornication so despicable that he allows it as grounds for divorce. (For a discussion of what fornication involves, refer to Chapter 9, paragraph 7, where fornication is explained.) Jehovah grants the innocent mate the right to decide whether to remain with the guilty partner or to seek a divorce. (Matthew 19:9) Hence, if an innocent mate decides to seek a divorce, that one does not take a step that Jehovah hates. At the same time, however, the Christian congregation does not encourage anyone to seek a divorce. In fact, some circumstances may move the innocent mate to remain with the guilty one, especially if that one is genuinely repentant. In the end, though, those who have a Scriptural basis for divorce must make their own decision and accept whatever consequences it may bring.—Galatians 6:5.

In certain *extreme* situations, some Christians have decided to separate from or divorce a marriage mate even though that one has not committed fornication. In such a case, the Bible stipulates that the departing one "remain unmarried or else make up again." (1 Corinthians 7:11) Such a Christian is not free to pursue a third party with a view to remarriage. (Matthew 5:32) Consider here a few exceptional situations that some have viewed as a basis for separation.

Willful nonsupport. A family may become destitute, lacking the basic essentials of life, because the husband fails to provide for them, although being able to do so. The Bible states: "If anyone does not provide for . . . members of his household, he has disowned the faith and is worse than a person without faith." (1 Timothy 5:8) If such a man refuses to change his ways, the wife would have to decide whether she needs to protect her welfare and that of her children by obtaining a legal separation. Of course,